WOODROW WILSON

WOODROW WILSON

J. Perry Leavell, Jr.

1987
CHELSEA HOUSE PUBLISHERS
NEW YORK
NEW HAVEN   PHILADELPHIA

EDITORIAL DIRECTOR: Nancy Toff
SENIOR EDITOR: John W. Selfridge
ASSOCIATE EDITOR: Marian W. Taylor
MANAGING EDITOR: Karyn Gullen Browne
COPY CHIEF: Perry King
EDITORIAL STAFF: Maria Behan, Karen Dreste,
          Pierre Hauser, Kathleen McDermott,
          Howard Ratner, Alma Rodriguez,
          Bert Yaeger
PICTURE EDITOR: Elizabeth Terhune
PICTURE RESEARCH: Brian Araujo
ART DIRECTOR: Giannella Garrett
LAYOUT: Irene Friedman
ART ASSISTANTS: Noreen Lamb, Carol McDougall,
          Victoria Tomaselli
COVER ILLUSTRATION: Frank Steiner

CREATIVE DIRECTOR: Harold Steinberg

Frontispiece courtesy of The Bettmann Archive

First Printing

Library of Congress Cataloging in Publication Data

Leavell, Perry. WOODROW WILSON.

(World leaders past & present)
Bibliography: p.
Includes index.
1. Wilson, Woodrow, 1856–1924— Juvenile literature.
2. Presidents—United States—Biography—Juvenile
literature. [1. Wilson, Woodrow, 1856–1924. 2. Presidents]
I. Title. II. Series.
E767.L52   1987   973.91′3′0924 [B] [92]   86-24463
ISBN 0-87754-557-X

Contents

ADENAUER
ALEXANDER THE GREAT
MARC ANTONY
KING ARTHUR
ATATÜRK
ATTLEE
BEGIN
BEN-GURION
BISMARCK
LÉON BLUM
BOLÍVAR
CESARE BORGIA
BRANDT
BREZHNEV
CAESAR
CALVIN
CASTRO
CATHERINE THE GREAT
CHARLEMAGNE
CHIANG KAI-SHEK
CHURCHILL
CLEMENCEAU
CLEOPATRA
CORTÉS
CROMWELL
DANTON
DE GAULLE
DE VALERA
DISRAELI
EISENHOWER
ELEANOR OF AQUITAINE
QUEEN ELIZABETH I
FERDINAND AND ISABELLA
FRANCO

FREDERICK THE GREAT
INDIRA GANDHI
MOHANDAS GANDHI
GARIBALDI
GENGHIS KHAN
GLADSTONE
GORBACHEV
HAMMARSKJÖLD
HENRY VIII
HENRY OF NAVARRE
HINDENBURG
HITLER
HO CHI MINH
HUSSEIN
IVAN THE TERRIBLE
ANDREW JACKSON
JEFFERSON
JOAN OF ARC
POPE JOHN XXIII
LYNDON JOHNSON
JUÁREZ
JOHN F. KENNEDY
KENYATTA
KHOMEINI
KHRUSHCHEV
MARTIN LUTHER KING, JR.
KISSINGER
LENIN
LINCOLN
LLOYD GEORGE
LOUIS XIV
LUTHER
JUDAS MACCABEUS
MAO ZEDONG

MARY, QUEEN OF SCOTS
GOLDA MEIR
METTERNICH
MUSSOLINI
NAPOLEON
NASSER
NEHRU
NERO
NICHOLAS II
NIXON
NKRUMAH
PERICLES
PERÓN
QADDAFI
ROBESPIERRE
ELEANOR ROOSEVELT
FRANKLIN D. ROOSEVELT
THEODORE ROOSEVELT
SADAT
STALIN
SUN YAT-SEN
TAMERLANE
THATCHER
TITO
TROTSKY
TRUDEAU
TRUMAN
VICTORIA
WASHINGTON
WEIZMANN
WOODROW WILSON
XERXES
ZHOU ENLAI

ON LEADERSHIP
Arthur M. Schlesinger, jr.

LEADERSHIP, it may be said, is really what makes the world go round. Love no doubt smooths the passage; but love is a private transaction between consenting adults. Leadership is a public transaction with history. The idea of leadership affirms the capacity of individuals to move, inspire, and mobilize masses of people so that they act together in pursuit of an end. Sometimes leadership serves good purposes, sometimes bad; but whether the end is benign or evil, great leaders are those men and women who leave their personal stamp on history.

Now, the very concept of leadership implies the proposition that individuals can make a difference. This proposition has never been universally accepted. From classical times to the present day, eminent thinkers have regarded individuals as no more than the agents and pawns of larger forces, whether the gods and goddesses of the ancient world or, in the modern era, race, class, nation, the dialectic, the will of the people, the spirit of the times, history itself. Against such forces, the individual dwindles into insignificance.

So contends the thesis of historical determinism. Tolstoy's great novel *War and Peace* offers a famous statement of the case. Why, Tolstoy asked, did millions of men in the Napoleonic wars, denying their human feelings and their common sense, move back and forth across Europe slaughtering their fellows? "The war," Tolstoy answered, "was bound to happen simply because it was bound to happen." All prior history predetermined it. As for leaders, they, Tolstoy said, "are but the labels that serve to give a name to an end and, like labels, they have the least possible connection with the event." The greater the leader, "the more conspicuous the inevitability and the predestination of every act he commits." The leader, said Tolstoy, is "the slave of history."

Determinism takes many forms. Marxism is the determinism of class. Nazism the determinism of race. But the idea of men and women as the slaves of history runs athwart the deepest human instincts. Rigid determinism abolishes the idea of human freedom—

the assumption of free choice that underlies every move we make, every word we speak, every thought we think. It abolishes the idea of human responsibility, since it is manifestly unfair to reward or punish people for actions that are by definition beyond their control. No one can live consistently by any deterministic creed. The Marxist states prove this themselves by their extreme susceptibility to the cult of leadership.

More than that, history refutes the idea that individuals make no difference. In December 1931 a British politician crossing Park Avenue in New York City between 76th and 77th Streets around 10:30 P.M. looked in the wrong direction and was knocked down by an automobile—a moment, he later recalled, of a man aghast, a world aglare: "I do not understand why I was not broken like an eggshell or squashed like a gooseberry." Fourteen months later an American politician, sitting in an open car in Miami, Florida, was fired on by an assassin; the man beside him was hit. Those who believe that individuals make no difference to history might well ponder whether the next two decades would have been the same had Mario Constasino's car killed Winston Churchill in 1931 and Giuseppe Zangara's bullet killed Franklin Roosevelt in 1933. Suppose, in addition, that Adolf Hitler had been killed in the street fighting during the Munich *Putsch* of 1923 and that Lenin had died of typhus during World War I. What would the 20th century be like now?

For better or for worse, individuals do make a difference. "The notion that a people can run itself and its affairs anonymously," wrote the philosopher William James, "is now well known to be the silliest of absurdities. Mankind does nothing save through initiatives on the part of inventors, great or small, and imitation by the rest of us—these are the sole factors in human progress. Individuals of genius show the way, and set the patterns, which common people then adopt and follow."

Leadership, James suggests, means leadership in thought as well as in action. In the long run, leaders in thought may well make the greater difference to the world. But, as Woodrow Wilson once said, "Those only are leaders of men, in the general eye, who lead in action. . . . It is at their hands that new thought gets its translation into the crude language of deeds." Leaders in thought often invent in solitude and obscurity, leaving to later generations the tasks of imitation. Leaders in action—the leaders portrayed in this series—have to be effective in their own time.

And they cannot be effective by themselves. They must act in response to the rhythms of their age. Their genius must be adapted, in a phrase of William James's, "to the receptivities of the moment." Leaders are useless without followers. "There goes the mob," said the French politician hearing a clamor in the streets. "I am their leader. I must follow them." Great leaders turn the inchoate emotions of the mob to purposes of their own. They seize on the opportunities of their time, the hopes, fears, frustrations, crises, potentialities. They succeed when events have prepared the way for them, when the community is awaiting to be aroused, when they can provide the clarifying and organizing ideas. Leadership ignites the circuit between the individual and the mass and thereby alters history.

It may alter history for better or for worse. Leaders have been responsible for the most extravagant follies and most monstrous crimes that have beset suffering humanity. They have also been vital in such gains as humanity has made in individual freedom, religious and racial tolerance, social justice and respect for human rights.

There is no sure way to tell in advance who is going to lead for good and who for evil. But a glance at the gallery of men and women in *World Leaders—Past and Present* suggests some useful tests.

One test is this: do leaders lead by force or by persuasion? By command or by consent? Through most of history leadership was exercised by the divine right of authority. The duty of followers was to defer and to obey. "Theirs not to reason why,/ Theirs but to do and die." On occasion, as with the so-called "enlightened despots" of the 18th century in Europe, absolutist leadership was animated by humane purposes. More often, absolutism nourished the passion for domination, land, gold and conquest and resulted in tyranny.

The great revolution of modern times has been the revolution of equality. The idea that all people should be equal in their legal condition has undermined the old structure of authority, hierarchy and deference. The revolution of equality has had two contrary effects on the nature of leadership. For equality, as Alexis de Tocqueville pointed out in his great study *Democracy in America*, might mean equality in servitude as well as equality in freedom.

"I know of only two methods of establishing equality in the political world," Tocqueville wrote. "Rights must be given to every citizen, or none at all to anyone . . . save one, who is the master of all." There was no middle ground "between the sovereignty of all and the absolute power of one man." In his astonishing prediction of 20th-century totalitarian dictatorship, Tocqueville explained how the revolution of equality could lead to the *"Führerprinzip"* and more terrible absolutism than the world had ever known.

But when rights are given to every citizen and the sovereignty of all is established, the problem of leadership takes a new form, becomes more exacting than ever before. It is easy to issue commands and enforce them by the rope and the stake, the concentration camp and the *gulag.* It is much harder to use argument and achievement to overcome opposition and win consent. The Founding Fathers of the United States understood the difficulty. They believed that history had given them the opportunity to decide, as Alexander Hamilton wrote in the first Federalist Paper, whether men are indeed capable of basing government on "reflection and choice, or whether they are forever destined to depend . . . on accident and force."

Government by reflection and choice called for a new style of leadership and a new quality of followership. It required leaders to be responsive to popular concerns, and it required followers to be active and informed participants in the process. Democracy does not eliminate emotion from politics; sometimes it fosters demagoguery; but it is confident that, as the greatest of democratic leaders put it, you cannot fool all of the people all of the time. It measures leadership by results and retires those who overreach or falter or fail.

It is true that in the long run despots are measured by results too. But they can postpone the day of judgment, sometimes indefinitely, and in the meantime they can do infinite harm. It is also true that democracy is no guarantee of virtue and intelligence in government, for the voice of the people is not necessarily the voice of God. But democracy, by assuring the right of opposition, offers built-in resistance to the evils inherent in absolutism. As the theologian Reinhold Niebuhr summed it up, "Man's capacity for justice makes democracy possible, but man's inclination to injustice makes democracy necessary."

A second test for leadership is the end for which power is sought. When leaders have as their goal the supremacy of a master race or the promotion of totalitarian revolution or the acquisition and exploitation of colonies or the protection of greed and privilege or the preservation of personal power, it is likely that their leadership will do little to advance the cause of humanity. When their goal is the abolition of slavery, the liberation of women, the enlargement of opportunity for the poor and powerless, the extension of equal rights to racial minorities, the defense of the freedoms of expression and opposition, it is likely that their leadership will increase the sum of human liberty and welfare.

Leaders have done great harm to the world. They have also conferred great benefits. You will find both sorts in this series. Even "good" leaders must be regarded with a certain wariness. Leaders are not demigods; they put on their trousers one leg after another just like ordinary mortals. No leader is infallible, and every leader needs to be reminded of this at regular intervals. Irreverence irritates leaders but is their salvation. Unquestioning submission corrupts leaders and demands followers. Making a cult of a leader is always a mistake. Fortunately hero worship generates its own antidote. "Every hero," said Emerson, "becomes a bore at last."

The signal benefit the great leaders confer is to embolden the rest of us to live according to our own best selves, to be active, insistent, and resolute in affirming our own sense of things. For great leaders attest to the reality of human freedom against the supposed inevitabilities of history. And they attest to the wisdom and power that may lie within the most unlikely of us, which is why Abraham Lincoln remains the supreme example of great leadership. A great leader, said Emerson, exhibits new possibilities to all humanity. "We feed on genius. . . . Great men exist that there may be greater men."

Great leaders, in short, justify themselves by emancipating and empowering their followers. So humanity struggles to master its destiny, remembering with Alexis de Tocqueville: "It is true that around every man a fatal circle is traced beyond which he cannot pass; but within the wide verge of that circle he is powerful and free; as it is with man, so with communities."

—*New York*

1

America Declares War

On the evening of April 2, 1917, American President Woodrow Wilson left the White House and, escorted by a troop of mounted soldiers, headed for the Capitol. Thousands of people lined his route; they cheered and waved small American flags as the president passed by. A light spring rain fell from the darkening sky, but the Capitol's white dome gleamed in its bath of floodlights.

Wilson had been reelected president a few months earlier. In Europe, a vast and bloody conflict was in progress; on one side were Great Britain, France, and Russia, and on the other, Germany and its allies. Wilson's campaign had featured such slogans as "He kept us out of war" and "War in the East, Peace in the West, Thank God for Wilson." He had promised to keep the United States out of the conflict. Now he was about to ask Congress for a declaration of war against Germany.

Wilson had agonized over this move; he detested the use of violence as a means of solving interna-

> *The world must be made safe for democracy. Civilization itself seems to be in the balance. But the right is more precious than peace.*
> —WOODROW WILSON
> asking Congress for a declaration of war in 1917

British soldiers carry a wounded comrade to a base hospital in France. As World War I increased in fury, it became clear to Woodrow Wilson that, despite his 1916 campaign promises, the United States could not remain neutral in the conflict.

A 1916 Wilson campaign truck is festooned with flags and posters proclaiming the candidate's platform. The subtle combination of peace *and* preparedness led to Republican charges that Wilson was secretly planning to enter the war.

tional disputes. Contradictory as it sounds, he was going to propose war for only one reason: to obtain and keep peace. When he stood before Congress, he asserted that war had been "thrust upon" the United States by the actions of Germany. He said the United States had "no quarrel with the German people"; America's enemy was Germany's "irresponsible government," which had "thrown aside all considerations of humanity and of right" and was "running amok."

Wilson reminded his listeners of his efforts to keep the United States out of the war. He talked about the four American ships that had been sunk by German submarines in the preceding few weeks, and about the American lives that had been lost. (German submarines had also been responsible for the sinking of the *Lusitania*, a British liner that went down off the coast of Ireland in 1915; 128 of the 1,198 people who died on the *Lusitania* had been Americans.)

Now, asserted Wilson, "neutrality is no longer feasible or desirable," (though the United States had for some time been shipping munitions to Germany's enemies — not entirely neutral). He said the United States should enter into war not in a spirit of revenge, but in a spirit of idealism. "The world," he declared, "must be made safe for democracy." He concluded, "It is a fearful thing to lead this great peaceful people into war, into the most terrible and disastrous of all wars, civilization itself seeming to be in the balance. But the right is more precious than peace. . . ."

Wilson left the Capitol to the sound of enthusiastic applause. "Think what it was they were applauding," he wrote afterward. "My message today was a message of death for our young men. How strange it seems to applaud that."

By April 6, 1917, Congress had voted overwhelmingly for war. Woodrow Wilson had made the fateful decisions that led to American participation in the war; now he would lead the nation through one of the most traumatic periods in its history. By the time the conflict — known at the time as the "Great War," and later as World War I — ended 18 months

> *We have no selfish end to serve. We desire no conquest, no dominion. We seek no indemnities for ourselves, no material compensation for the sacrifice we shall freely make.*
> —WOODROW WILSON asking Congress for a declaration of war, April 2, 1917

Wilson asks Congress for a declaration of war on Germany on April 2, 1917. Two days later, the Senate passed the declaration by a vote of 82 to 6; on April 6 the House concurred by a vote of 373 to 50. Wilson signed it the same day.

later, Wilson was more than a president of the United States. In the debates about the peace treaties that would shape postwar society, he had become a world leader.

Winston Churchill, who would serve as Great Britain's prime minister during World War II, commented on Wilson's influence on world events at this time. "The action of the United States, with its repercussions on the history of the world, depended," said Churchill, "upon the workings of this man's mind and spirit to the exclusion of almost every other factor. . . . He played a part in the fate of nations incomparably more direct and personal than any other man."

A *New York Times* "extra" announces the sinking of the *Lusitania* by a German submarine on May 7, 1915. The Germans claimed that the British liner had been carrying munitions for the Allies, a charge verified by recently uncovered documents.

The New York Times.

"All the News That's Fit to Print."

EXTRA
5:30 A.M.

VOL. LXIV ... NO. 20,923. ..... NEW YORK, SATURDAY, MAY 8, 1915.—TWENTY-FOUR PAGES. ..... ONE CENT .....

LUSITANIA SUNK BY A SUBMARINE, PROBABLY 1,260 DEAD; TWICE TORPEDOED OFF IRISH COAST; SINKS IN 15 MINUTES; CAPT. TURNER SAVED, FROHMAN AND VANDERBILT MISSING; WASHINGTON BELIEVES THAT A GRAVE CRISIS IS AT HAND

The Lost Cunard Steamship Lusitania
X Where the First Torpedo Struck.   XX Where the Second Torpedo Struck.

2

President of Princeton

Thomas Woodrow Wilson was born in Staunton, Virginia, on December 28, 1856. He was the son, grandson, and nephew of Presbyterian ministers. His father, Joseph Ruggles Wilson, a teacher as well as a clergyman, moved his family several times while "Tommy" Wilson was growing up. They lived in Augusta, Georgia; Columbia, South Carolina; and Wilmington, North Carolina.

Wilson would later say that his father was "the best instructor, the most inspiring companion . . . that a youngster ever had." Joseph Wilson encouraged his son to think deeply about religion and politics, and he helped him polish his writing and speaking skills. Tommy's mother, Janet "Jessie" Woodrow Wilson, raised him and his three siblings with love and firmness. She was pleased when her son, after graduating from college, decided to drop his nickname. "I always wanted to call you Woodrow," she said.

Young Wilson was not a quick learner. He was 9 years old before he mastered the alphabet and 11 by the time he learned to read well. His parents were

When young Tommy Wilson sat in the pew and heard his father bring the Word to the people, he was watching the model upon which his career was to be fashioned. He never aspired to be a clergyman, but he made politics his means of spreading spiritual enlightenment, of expressing the powerful Protestant urge for "service" upon which he had been reared.
—RICHARD HOFSTADTER
American historian

Wilson, pictured here in his academic robes, was named president of Princeton University in 1902. Although he had gained a national reputation for his scholarly writing, he was surprised by his appointment to the college presidency; it came, he said, like "a thunderbolt out of a clear sky."

defensive and embarrassed in front of other family members because of their son's slowness in school. Many of today's historians believe Wilson suffered from a form of dyslexia, a common learning disability that was little understood at the time. Dyslexia occurs in people at all levels of intelligence and in all social and economic groups. (Another dyslexic well known in politics was millionaire Nelson Rockefeller, who served as governor of New York and vice-president under Gerald Ford.)

Since no one understood the difficulties the boy faced, he struggled with his problems alone. Gradually, he learned how to deal with them. He never

Woodrow Wilson's parents, Janet and Joseph Ruggles Wilson. Native Ohioans, the Wilsons had moved to the South as Joseph pursued his dual career of teacher and Presbyterian minister.

was able to read easily, but he developed strong powers of concentration and a near-photographic memory. When he was 16, he taught himself shorthand as a way of compensating for his poor handwriting. Later, he bought one of the recently invented typewriters, eventually becoming a skilled typist. Wilson's struggle with his learning handicap must have caused him pain, but it probably also contributed to his strong personality and character. In future times of crisis he would have reserves of strength on which to draw.

Wilson's childhood was punctuated by the Civil War, which began when he was five years old. "My

Wilson spent the first years of his life in this house in Staunton, Virginia.

earliest recollection," he once said, "is of standing at my father's gateway in Augusta, Georgia, when I was four years old, and hearing someone pass and say that Mr. Lincoln was elected and there was to be war."

He saw wounded soldiers in his father's church and heard terrifying reports about Union General William T. Sherman's bloody march through Georgia and South Carolina. Among the legacies of his southern upbringing were a hatred of war and a deep faith in the Democratic party. Wilson looked forward to a future in which southerners would once more play a great role in national politics, but he could never have guessed that he himself would be the first southerner elected to the presidency after the Civil War.

Wilson was interested in politics from an early age. When he was a teenager he decorated his room

with a picture of British Prime Minister William Gladstone, and he often joked with friends about his ambition to become a United States senator.

In 1873 he enrolled at Davidson College, a Presbyterian institution in North Carolina. Two years later, he entered the College of New Jersey in Princeton (known after 1896 as Princeton University). His parents hoped he would train for the ministry, but the young man had other plans. Although he remained deeply religious all his life, he had no desire to carry on the family tradition by becoming a clergyman. In college he was popular with his fellow students and active in extracurricular activities, especially in public speaking and as editor of the student newspaper, the *Princetonian*.

His grades placed him in the top third of his class. His best subject was history; his worst was science. Especially interested in government and public affairs, he eagerly studied scholarly books about the U.S. Constitution and the British parliamentary system, which he came to believe was the best form of government in the world.

Wilson graduated from college in 1879. He wanted to enter politics; he decided to study law in preparation for a political career. He attended the University of Virginia Law School and in 1882 began practicing law in Atlanta, Georgia. He soon found that he detested working as a lawyer. He also came to the conclusion that, without money and connections, his chances for success in the political arena were slim. He decided to start all over again.

His new ambition was to become a college professor of government and political science. In a letter to a friend, he confided that while his "deepest secret" was still his hope of having "a statesman's career," he was willing to settle for teaching and writing about the subject he loved. In 1883, at the age of 26, he returned to college. This time, it was the graduate school at Johns Hopkins University in Baltimore, Maryland, where he signed up for courses in government and history.

In the spring before he entered Johns Hopkins, Wilson met Ellen Louise Axson, a young woman from Savannah, Georgia. Like himself, she was the

> *An idealist, a philosopher, a moralist, a religionist, he was born; as someone has well said, halfway between the Bible and the dictionary, and he never lost his faith in the power of words.*
> —THOMAS A. BAILEY
> American historian, on Wilson

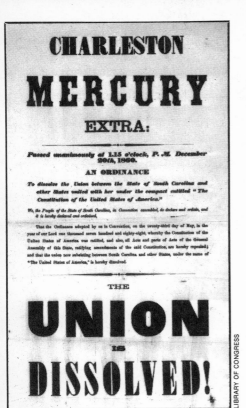

The Charleston (S.C.) *Mercury* of December 20, 1860, reprinted South Carolina's resolution to secede from the United States, a move that heralded the Civil War. Wilson's childhood memories of the war's carnage probably contributed to his ardent pacifism as an adult.

When Abraham Lincoln, 16th president of the United States, took office in 1860, Woodrow Wilson, who would be the nation's 28th president, was four years old. One of Wilson's earliest memories was of hearing that Lincoln had been elected.

child of a Presbyterian minister, and she loved books. The two were immediately attracted to each other; by September 1883 they were engaged.

At Johns Hopkins, Wilson was a whirlwind of activity. He studied history and international law, learned German, joined the college literary society, sang with the glee club, and wrote a book, *Congressional Government*. Dealing with political leadership in America, the book was published to high critical praise in January 1885. The following June, Wilson and Ellen Axson were married.

Wilson got a job teaching history and political economy at Bryn Mawr, a women's college near Philadelphia, Pennsylvania. He and his wife moved there in September. For the first time in his life, Wilson, now 28 years old, was financially independent of his parents. Margaret, the first of the Wilsons' three daughters, was born in April 1886. (Jessie would arrive in 1887, Eleanor in 1889).

Wilson stayed at Bryn Mawr for three years, but he was never entirely happy about teaching women,

whose imaginations he found earthbound. When Wesleyan University, a men's school in Middletown, Connecticut, offered him a professorship in 1888, he accepted it quickly. At Wesleyan, Wilson taught courses in history and government, coached the football team, and started a student debating club. He was happy in his new situation, but two years later, he received an offer impossible to resist: a teaching position at his alma mater, the College of New Jersey in Princeton.

Wilson had once remarked to Ellen that college lectures were often dull because the teachers lacked imagination and the ability to inspire students. "Perfunctory lecturing," he had said, "is of no service in the world." Wilson was no "perfunctory" (routine and uninspired) speaker. Burning with enthusiasm, he ignited his listeners at the College of New Jersey with excitement about such "heavy"

Wounded Confederate troops await medical attention in a Virginia field hospital in 1862. The Civil War was fought by young men; the majority of soldiers were under 21, and many were under the age of 15. More than 500,000 of the nation's 31 million citizens died in the course of the war.

Ellen Louise Axson, Wilson's first wife. Wilson first saw Axson in church, then slyly arranged to meet her father, who was — like his own — a Presbyterian minister. The young couple began courting immediately, and were married two years later, in 1885.

subjects as constitutional law, administration, and English common law. Students flocked to hear Professor Wilson, who became one of the most popular teachers in the history of the college.

As well as acquiring local fame, Wilson was beginning to become nationally known in academic circles. He had published several books, and he frequently wrote articles for scholarly magazines. Other prestigious universities began to offer him positions. Hoping to keep him in New Jersey, the college directors paid him a considerably higher salary than his colleagues.

The Wilsons were happy in Princeton. He was the toast of the campus; she presided over a handsome house, three daughters, and a full social life. The

Ellen and Woodrow Wilson are joined by their daughters, Margaret, Jessie, and Eleanor, during a New Hampshire summer vacation. Unlike many Victorian fathers, Wilson was a warm and affectionate parent who often played with his children and read aloud to them.

During his term as president of Princeton University, Wilson lived with his family in an elegant home known as "Prospect." The scene of many official receptions, the mansion was also the setting for high-spirited gatherings of the Wilson clan.

Wilson home was usually overflowing with visiting relatives and the sound of laughter. In an era when many fathers expected their children to be "seen but not heard," Woodrow Wilson engaged in raucous games with his youngsters, and often read aloud to them before bedtime.

One incident marred the family's contentment. In 1896 Wilson suffered what was probably a small stroke — a burst blood vessel in the brain. The stroke produced a lack of flexibility in Wilson's right hand, but no major problems at the time. It was, however, an indication that serious medical troubles might be in store.

During his 12 years in Princeton, Wilson published 35 articles and 9 books, including a biography of George Washington and *History of the American People*, a scholarly work in five volumes. He also taught courses at important law schools, and gave well-attended lectures around the country. Partly as a result of his popularity with his students, fellow faculty members, and powerful alumni, and partly because of his national reputation as a

scholar, Wilson was named president of Princeton University in 1902. He was the first layman to hold that position; all his predecessors had been ministers.

Wilson's eight years as president were devoted to making Princeton one of the great universities in the country. He requested — and received — unheard-of sums of money from the college trustees to hire distinguished professors and construct new classrooms and laboratories.

The new president also instituted a number of reforms. One of them was to upgrade the quality of the students by significantly raising entrance requirements. At one point, he was asked to admit an applicant who had failed the entrance examinations. Wilson flatly refused. "I want you to understand," he thundered, "that if the angel Gabriel applied for admission to Princeton University and could not pass the entrance examinations, he would not be admitted!"

Socialist leader Eugene V. Debs, one of Wilson's opponents in the presidential election of 1912, ran for president five times between 1900 and 1920. In 1912, the Socialists received six percent of the vote, the highest total in the party's history.

The air currents of the world never ventilated his mind.
—WALTER HINES PAGE
American journalist and
diplomat, on Wilson

Wilson ordered a revision of the curriculum, insisting that all students take certain required courses and demanding that they master their studies. "I am not going to propose that we compel the undergraduates to work all the time," he said, "but I am going to propose that we make the undergraduates want to work all the time."

Wilson's best-known reform was the introduction of the "preceptorial" system of teaching. This meant that, instead of sitting in huge lecture halls and simply listening to professors, students divided up into small groups. Here, they were taught by young teachers who allowed them to talk and ask questions. Wilson himself interviewed and hired these instructors, or preceptors.

Reform and change can produce opposition. As time went on, more and more of Wilson's proposals came under attack. Some, like his plan to abolish

Young laborers work in an Indiana factory in 1908. Children in early 20th-century America, where child-labor laws were nonexistent, often worked 14-hour shifts. The first federal legislation regulating the work of children was passed by the Wilson administration in 1916.

Somber and pensive, the president of Princeton University walks alone on the campus. Wilson thoroughly enjoyed most of the eight years he spent as head of the prestigious college, but the final months of his presidency were marred by heavy criticism of the reforms he had instituted.

the upperclassmen's eating clubs (which were similar to fraternities on other campuses), were not always planned carefully. They drew heavy fire, particularly from alumni. Like most of us, Wilson did not like criticism. He sometimes forgot that good people may disagree with one another without becoming enemies, and he sometimes responded to criticism of his programs by attacking his critics personally.

Wilson was becoming increasingly discouraged and depressed by the infighting and bickering that was now part of his university experience. When he was offered the chance to fulfill his old dream by entering politics, he jumped at the chance. Larger worlds awaited him.

3

From Princeton to Washington

At country fairs and picnics, Americans of the 19th and early 20th centuries tested their muscles, agility, and luck at a variety of games and contests. One popular activity was watching a group of dirty, loud young men try to catch a greased pig. American satirist Ambrose Bierce once defined the American presidency as "the greased pig in the field game of American politics." Certainly the election of a president evoked a circuslike atmosphere and was often accompanied by loud, sometimes profane, squealing from participants and onlookers alike.

Woodrow Wilson was offered the chance to enter politics in 1910. The story behind that offer had begun on a sunny day in October 1902, when J. P. Morgan gave his friend George Harvey a ride in his luxurious private railroad car. Morgan was a railroad tycoon and financier, a millionaire many times over; Harvey was the editor of the conservative magazine *Harper's Weekly*; the train's destination was Princeton, New Jersey.

In Princeton, the two men heard Wilson deliver his first speech as president of the university. They

> *I have always been among those who believed that the greatest freedom of speech was the greatest safety, because if a man is a fool, the best thing to do is encourage him to advertise the fact by speaking.*
> —WOODROW WILSON

When Wilson was named as a potential candidate for New Jersey's governorship in 1910, he said, "I will not accept the nomination unless it comes unanimously." Because of this condition, he would later be able to claim he had no obligations to any political machine.

were impressed. Harvey was soon telling friends that Wilson would "make a good president of the United States." The powerful editor was a member of the Democratic party, but he was extremely conservative. He and his equally right-wing political associates believed Wilson to be as conservative as themselves. They also saw him as respectable, electable, and malleable. In other words, they believed that his dignity and academic credentials would appeal to voters tired of flamboyant political showmen — and they thought that, once elected to office, he would follow their orders.

Before trying for the White House, of course, Wilson would have to enter politics at a somewhat lower level. In the years that followed Harvey's visit to Princeton, the editor tirelessly boosted Wilson as a candidate for the U.S. Senate and as a potential candidate for president. In 1906 he even ran a slogan at the top of each issue of the widely read *Harper's Weekly*: "For President — Woodrow Wilson." A year later, he hired an assistant to work full-time on promoting Wilson for political office.

Harvey and the other conservatives in the Democratic party regarded Wilson as a candidate who could weaken the influence of their political archenemy, William Jennings Bryan. Bryan, who had run for president on the Democratic ticket three times — and lost three times — was an immensely popular midwestern politician and spokesman for America's farmers. He was famous for his attacks on big business, the railroads in particular.

Not surprisingly, business interests in the Democratic party regarded Bryan as a dangerous radical, and they were eager to prevent him from being once again nominated for the presidency. Wilson, they thought, was just the man they needed.

Furthermore, many of Wilson's ideas genuinely appealed to Harvey and his friends. In his books and articles, Wilson had often displayed hostility to reformers and rebels. His treatment of radical movements in American history and of those who challenged current, conventional ideas and institutions was highly critical. His books sometimes expressed a low opinion of recent immigrants, and his

speeches reflected a commitment to the economic principle of *laissez faire* (non-interference by the state in economic affairs).

Wilson had often criticized labor unions, and he referred to the "crude and ignorant minds" of the farmers who supported Bryan in the 1890s. He had even said, in a 1907 letter to a friend, "Would that we could do something at once dignified and effective to knock Mr. Bryan once and for all into a cocked hat!"

Wilson, then, seemed like the ideal candidate to the conservative eastern wing of the Democratic party. In 1910 George Harvey approached the leader of the New Jersey Democratic party, James Smith, and suggested that the party run Woodrow Wilson for governor.

Smith knew that, to survive, the Democratic party needed new leaders. Too many New Jersey voters believed — with some justice — that the Democrats were dominated by corrupt political bosses. Only by nominating new candidates who appeared independent and honest could the Democrats prove

Popular Nebraska politican William Jennings Bryan, a magnificent orator, campaigns for the presidency in 1896. Bryan first opposed, then supported, Wilson's bid for the presidential nomination in 1912. Wilson subsequently named him secretary of state.

"Breaker boys" — youngsters who picked shale out of huge piles of broken-up coal — peer forlornly from a Pennsylvania mine in 1911. The conservative politicians who backed Wilson's entry into politics opposed laws to protect such children, but Wilson was eventually to support child-labor legislation.

they deserved public support. Smith knew the voters would be impressed by Wilson's reputation for integrity. He fully expected, however, that if Wilson was elected, he would accept the control of the bosses.

In June 1910 Smith and Harvey asked Wilson to run for governor of New Jersey. They told him they believed he could not only be elected, but that he could go on to higher office. After Harvey's long and enthusiastic boosting of his candidacy, Wilson could not have been surprised, but he must have been delighted. He had, after all, dreamed almost all his life of taking an active role in politics. He took a week to think it over, and then he said yes. Soon afterward, he resigned as president of Princeton.

Wilson was formally nominated for governor at the state Democratic convention in Trenton, New Jersey, in September 1910. The secretary of the convention introduced him enthusiastically as "the candidate for the governorship, and the next president of the United States."

Wilson's nomination had been strongly opposed by the liberal, or "progressive" wing of the party, who were also known as "insurgents." When the new candidate rose to make his acceptance speech, the insurgents scowled unhappily. But they were electrified by what they heard next. Wilson said that if he won the governorship, he would take on the job "with absolutely no pledge of any kind to prevent me from serving the people of the state."

The conservatives probably smiled to themselves, believing not a word of this. The progressives, however, were infused with hope. A young man in the audience named Joe Tumulty, who would soon become Wilson's secretary, was converted on the spot: "Thank God!" he shouted out. "At last a leader has come!"

Wilson quickly realized that if he hoped to win, he would have to conduct a campaign pledged to reform. The reform movement was wholeheartedly backed by the progressives and by increasing numbers of uncommitted voters. The movement called for some government control of industry and for regulation of railroads and public utilities. Among

The hurricane of reform called Progressivism, which blew through all levels of American political and social life in the years between 1900 and 1917, was many things, but above all it was a response to the challenge of the city and the factory, an attempt to bring to heel the untamed forces which had almost reduced the American Dream to a mockery.
—CARL DEGLER
American historian

its other goals were the adoption of primary elections and the direct election of U.S. senators. (At this time, New Jersey's senators were selected by the state legislature.)

Soon after his nomination, Wilson began praising the progressives' ideas and attacking the very political machine to which he owed his nomination. "I am," he insisted, "and always have been, an insurgent." This was a rather strange claim, coming from a man who, until just before the election, had been one of the insurgents' harshest critics.

How can Wilson's sudden transformation from

Addie Laird, a 12-year-old spinner, takes a rare break in a Vermont cotton mill in 1910. Public exposure of the harsh labor conditions in many American factories — particularly in the New England textile industry — helped create a demand for laws to protect exploited workers like Addie.

NATIONAL ARCHIVES

conservative to progressive be explained? Was he guilty of hypocrisy, of changing his political position in order to win an election? Or was he acting in accordance with his conception of democracy, which held that political leaders were obliged to listen to the public, to respond to public opinion, and to promote the more enlightened of the public's goals?

Many contemporary historians believe that in his 1910 campaign, Wilson was for the first time displaying a skill that he would often demonstrate in the future. This was the ability to understand what a majority of citizens believed, and then to phrase those beliefs in his own eloquent words, using them to support policies he believed were important.

Wilson was new at politics, but he was getting a rapid education. At first he thought he could run for governor on a limited budget, making a few speeches at public meetings. Soon, however, he was busy raising a war chest (campaign funds) in order to finance numerous appearances before large crowds. His ideas were somewhat vague at the beginning, but as his campaign progressed, Wilson's thoughts about economic and social changes became sharper and his goals clearer. His audiences were becoming increasingly enthusiastic when he spoke out in favor of reform. Wilson's new vocation, politics, was teaching him new ways of viewing the world.

Wilson's ideas and beliefs had always been more complex than Harvey and other conservatives recognized. In some areas, he was a true conservative; in others, he was a progressive. His belief in democracy was strong, and measures like instituting direct election of senators were compatible with that belief. He had always distrusted political machines, an attitude that led to his efforts to weaken these centers of arbitrary power. His fervent progressivism may have been new, but its sources were deeply rooted.

Wilson won the election and became governor of New Jersey. Now he faced a major challenge: political boss James Smith wished to become a U.S. senator; since he had arranged Wilson's victory, he

Millionaire industrialist and financier J. P. Morgan was an early Wilson backer. Like other wealthy conservatives who favored the Princeton president, Morgan believed Wilson to be a staunch rightwinger. He and his friends were to discover they had been seriously mistaken.

Outgoing President Theodore Roosevelt and his hand-picked successor, William Howard Taft, look out from the White House porch in 1908. Soon disillusioned with Taft, Roosevelt entered the presidential race in 1912; his candidacy split the Republican vote and ensured the victory of Democrat Woodrow Wilson.

LIBRARY OF CONGRESS

A man can change one or two of his opinions for his own advantage and change them perfectly honestly, but when a man changes all the well considered opinions of a lifetime and changes them all at once for his own popular advantage it seems to me that he must lack in loyalty of conviction.

—HENRY CABOT LODGE
American politician and
author, on Wilson

expected the new governor to arrange for his seat in the Senate. This presented a dilemma. If Wilson helped Smith, he would lose the support of the progressives. If he did not help Smith, he would lose both Smith's support and that of the party regulars.

Wilson knew what he had to do. Defying the powerful political machine that had backed him, he declared his support for another man, James Martine. In the ensuing campaign, Wilson proved that he was speedily mastering the art of politics: Martine won, and Smith was defeated. "I pitied Smith at the last," said Wilson. "He wept, they say, as he admitted himself utterly beaten." Perhaps it is not surprising that a friend of Smith later described Wilson as "a liar and an ingrate."

No matter what the Smith faction thought, however, Wilson emerged from this struggle with a national reputation for courage. Here was a governor who was free of machine politics, who had shaken off the control of political bosses. Now that he had shown his political muscle, Wilson proceeded to wrest control of the state government from the surprised political bosses. He forced a sweeping program of progressive reforms through a reluctant legislature: a corrupt-practices law, strict state regulation of railroads and public utilities, a direct primary, and a law making employers liable for their workers' on-the-job injuries.

From the beginning of his governorship, Wilson set his sights on the presidency of the United States. As Wilson's political triumphs in New Jersey mounted, more and more people across the country began to regard him as the Democratic party's strongest and most effective leader. His new followers included both progressives and some conservative Democrats. By 1911 Wilson was widely regarded as a major candidate for the presidency in the following year's election.

Before he could run for president, however, he had to get the Democratic nomination, and this

I tell you the so-called radicalism of our times is simply the effort of nature to release the generous energies of our people.
—WOODROW WILSON

The Republican Convention of 1912, held in Chicago, was the scene of an epic political battle between incumbent President Taft and former president Roosevelt. When Taft won the presidential nomination, Roosevelt formed the Bull Moose party, killing the Republicans' chances of recapturing the White House.

proved to be no easy job. He had several strong competitors, the most formidable of whom was Champ Clark of Missouri, speaker of the House of Representatives. Clark was the favorite of the leaders of the Democratic party.

The 1912 Democratic convention, held in June, was remarkable for the number of ballots it took to select a candidate. Clark got more votes (440) than Wilson (324) on the first ballot, but to win the nomination, a candidate needed a two-thirds majority. During the week of furious politicking that followed, votes were begged, traded, demanded. William Jennings Bryan, despite past differences of opinion, decided to throw his support to Wilson. Little by little, more delegates switched their votes to the New Jersey progressive. Exhausted but jubilant, the

Wilson, the newly nominated Democratic presidential candidate, addresses an enthusiastic crowd on August 7, 1912. "We stand," he said, "in the presence of an awakened nation."

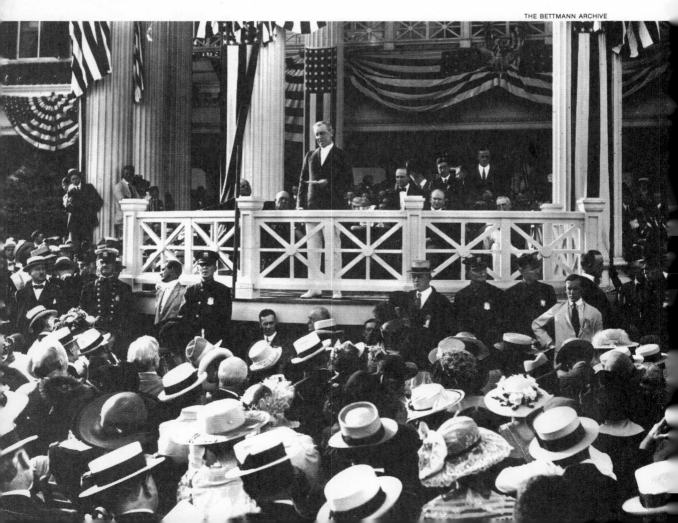

Democrats finally chose Wilson as their standard-bearer on the 46th ballot.

The election of 1912 was one of the most exciting in United States history. The dominant figure in the race was not Wilson, but Theodore Roosevelt, who had served as U.S. president from 1901 to 1909. Roosevelt, a charismatic and forceful leader, had become famous when he led his hard-fighting "Rough Riders" to victory in the 1898 Spanish-American War. He was one of the most colorful and popular political leaders the United States has ever produced.

Roosevelt had become increasingly disenchanted with the policies of his presidential successor, William Howard Taft. Progressives in the Republican party also considered Taft too conservative, and they encouraged Roosevelt to oppose him in 1912. At first Roosevelt resisted, but then he decided to seek the Republican party nomination. "My hat is in the ring!" he announced with characteristic verve. "The fight is on and I am stripped to the buff!"

Roosevelt was far more popular with the public than Taft, but the incumbent president nevertheless became the Republican party's candidate. Republican progressives then met in their own convention and nominated Roosevelt for the presidency. Roosevelt was in fine form, ready for a good fight. "We stand at Armageddon," he said at the convention, "and we battle for the Lord." He told newspaper reporters he was "feeling like a bull moose!" His Progressive party adopted this animal as their symbol and excitedly began to work for their man's election.

Discouraged by the strength of his adversaries and the public's indifference, Taft was hardly a contender. He sulked on the sidelines, complaining that he "might as well give up so far as being a candidate is concerned. There are so many people in the country who don't like me." He continued his half-hearted effort to be reelected largely to ensure Roosevelt's defeat.

The battle, then, was between Wilson the Democrat and Roosevelt the Republican-turned-Progressive. Roosevelt conducted a thunderous and

NATIONAL PORTRAIT GALLERY

Millionaire Andrew Carnegie merged his huge Carnegie Steel Company with several other major steel producers to form the United States Steel Corporation in 1901. This giant enterprise was typical of the powerful monopolies that Wilson promised to tame with antitrust legislation.

Shedding his habitual frostiness, Wilson ebulliently seeks votes during the 1912 election. The former professor's sharply honed campaign skills astonished many veteran political observers.

flamboyant campaign. Wilson was equally impassioned, but his public manner was more reserved; he appealed to voters' idealism rather than to their emotions. Wilson and Roosevelt's personal styles were far apart; their platforms, however, were not.

Roosevelt campaigned for what he called the "New Nationalism," Wilson for the "New Freedom." Both candidates endorsed such reforms as the direct election of senators and the right of women to vote, and both favored reducing the tremendous power that had come to rest in the hands of the nation's wealthy industrialists.

Most Americans had mixed feelings about the new corporate structures that had dominated the economy since the late 19th century. On the one hand, voters appreciated and boasted about the increased economic productivity and higher wages that the corporations seemed to make possible. On the other hand, they were alarmed by the vast economic and political power wielded by the owners and managers of these corporations. Cherished American political ideals seemed threatened. What would become of equality if economic "progress" brought poverty to some citizens? And what would become of democracy if millionaires acquired more power over the government than its elected officials had?

These were tough questions, and Wilson, who knew little about economics, needed help. He consulted with Louis D. Brandeis, a Boston lawyer and highly respected authority on large-scale economic problems. Brandeis helped Wilson clarify his position on big business.

Roosevelt was proposing to create a government commission to regulate the nation's giant corporations. Advised by Brandeis, Wilson said that Roosevelt's plan would merely lead to a larger and more expensive national government; it would not, said Wilson, cure or prevent the dangers posed by the huge companies' control of the nation's economy.

> *So long as governmental power existed exclusively for the king and not at all for the people, then the history of liberty was a history of the limitation of governmental power. But now the governmental power rests in the people, and the kings who enjoy privilege are the kings of the financial and industrial world.*
> —THEODORE ROOSEVELT
> American president
> (1901–09)

AP/WIDE WORLD PHOTOS

Louis Brandeis, a prominent liberal attorney, advised Wilson on his "trust-busting" legislation and formulated the powerful "Brandeis Brief," which supported the rights of laborers. In 1916 Wilson appointed Brandeis to the Supreme Court; he served as an associate justice until 1939.

Wilson addresses voters and reporters in Sea Girt, New Jersey. By the rough-and-tumble standards of the time, the 1912 campaign was not exceptionally nasty; Wilson's strongest attacks on Roosevelt and his supporters were somewhat sly references to "the third party."

American industry is not free, as once it was free; American enterprise is not free. Why? Because the laws of this country do not prevent the strong from crushing the weak.
—WOODROW WILSON

Wilson said the solution lay in the passage of laws that would prevent the strong from crushing the weak. He proposed to restore traditional competition among smaller businesses by breaking up massive corporations. Wilson's "New Freedom" promised big results at relatively small cost, and it envisaged less fundamental change than Roosevelt's program.

Roosevelt's reform proposals, then, were seen as more extreme than Wilson's. This put Wilson in a happy position: between Taft on his right and Roosevelt on his left. He criticized Taft for being too conservative and Roosevelt for being too radical; he remained in the center, where American voters are traditionally found.

Wilson proved to be an unexpectedly effective campaigner. He seemed to inspire his audiences, to make them proud of themselves and optimistic about the future. Even more unexpectedly, the dignified university leader found himself thoroughly enjoying his rough-and-tumble campaign appearances. The public clearly liked him, and he clearly enjoyed being liked. A remarkable intellectual and emotional rapport had sprung up between Wilson and the American voter.

Election Day, November 5, 1912, brought a decisive victory for Wilson. He received 6.3 million votes to Roosevelt's 4.1 million and Taft's 3.5 million. Although he won only 42 percent of the popular vote, Wilson gained an overwhelming majority of electoral college votes: 435 to Roosevelt's 88 and Taft's 8. Clearly, if the Republican party had remained united it would have won. But divide it did, giving the nation its first Democratic president since 1892. The big winner in 1912 was progressivism, for between them, Roosevelt and Wilson won more than two-thirds of the votes cast.

On election night Wilson addressed a crowd that gathered at his home to cheer his victory. "I myself have no feeling of triumph tonight," he said. "I have a feeling of solemn responsibility." The new president made it plain that he was determined "to square every process of our national life again with the standards we so proudly set up at the beginning and have always carried in our hearts."

One-term President William Howard Taft escorts his successor, President-elect Woodrow Wilson, to the Capitol for Wilson's March 4, 1913, inauguration. With Wilson's victory came a Democratic Congress, the first in many years and a sign of the nation's reformist mood.

4

President of the United States

No president ever had a clearer perception of the office than Woodrow Wilson had in 1913. In the words of political scientist Edward S. Corwin, "For the first time in its history the United States had a president who knew something about the functioning of political conditions abroad, and who had the intellect and skill to apply his knowledge to the stimulation and enrichment of the political process in this country."

Wilson had once believed that American presidents had little real power. In his book *Congressional Government*, he argued that Congress was the dominant branch of U.S. government and that within Congress, power was held by the committees and committee chairmen. It was they, he maintained, who secretly ran the government. His views had changed sharply by 1908, when he published *Constitutional Government in the United States.*

In this book, he conceded that the framers of the Constitution had held a relatively narrow view of presidential power. However, he said, changing circumstances had enlarged the president's role. As

> *We have been proud of our industrial achievements, but we have not hitherto stopped thoughtfully enough to count the human cost, the cost of lives snuffed out, of energies overtaxed and broken, the fearful physical and spiritual cost.*
> —WOODROW WILSON
> from his first inaugural address

Wilson addresses a rally on June 14, 1915, the 138th anniversary of the day the American flag was adopted by the Continental Congress of 1777. Wilson originated the idea of observing Flag Day, but it did not become a legal United States holiday until Congress gave it official status in 1949.

AP/WIDE WORLD PHOTOS

Joseph Tumulty, Wilson's private secretary, vacations at a Florida beach in 1930, six years after the death of his former boss. A powerful bond of affection, respect, and loyalty existed between Wilson and his long-time aide, who was one of Wilson's earliest political supporters.

the nation's economy and foreign policy had become more complicated, its citizens had "grown more and more inclined . . . to look to the president as the unifying force in our complex system, the leader both of his party and of the nation."

After observing Theodore Roosevelt in action, Wilson concluded that the office of the president is "anything he has the sagacity and force to make it. . . . The president is at liberty, both in law and conscience, to be as big a man as he can."

Wilson's actual political experience had been limited to his two-year stint as governor of New Jersey. Nevertheless, he had no doubts about his ability to lead the nation, as he indicated in his stirring inaugural address. "I summon all honest men, all patriotic, all forward-looking men, to my side," he said.

It is not men that interest or disturb me primarily, it is ideas. Ideas live; men die.
—WOODROW WILSON

"God helping me, I will not fail them, if they will but counsel and sustain me!" He canceled the traditional inaugural ball to indicate his seriousness.

Wilson knew how to dramatize issues and capture public attention. At the beginning of his term, he called a special joint session of Congress. Then he surprised everyone by appearing before the session to seek support for the bills he wanted passed. Not since Thomas Jefferson's day, more than a century earlier, had a president delivered his message to Congress in person. Wilson said he was glad to prove that the president was a human being, "not a mere department of the government hailing Congress from some isolated island of jealous power." Over the next eight years, he would often speak on the floor of Congress.

Wilson considered the British prime ministerial system a model of effective executive leadership.

Wilson, who once said that talking to Colonel Edward M. House was "like talking to myself," takes an autumn walk with his old friend and adviser. House had no formal government position, but Wilson relied heavily on his counsel, which gave the wealthy Texan a strong hand in shaping national affairs.

John D. Rockefeller's Standard Oil Company gave him virtual control of the oil business in the United States and much of the rest of the world. Portrayed by a contemporary cartoonist as a king, Rockefeller exemplified the millionaire industrialists whose awesome power Wilson's administration aimed to curb.

Just as the prime minister led Parliament, Wilson was determined to lead Congress. He often met with congressional leaders in the President's Room at the Capitol, a chamber little used by his predecessors. He had a special telephone line installed between the White House and the Capitol so he could reach legislators quickly when he wanted to talk to them.

Wilson insisted on party loyalty. Democrats could disagree with one another in private conferences, but once the majority had decided on a course of action, he expected all members of the party to vote unanimously.

"Power," said Wilson, "consists in one's capacity . . . to lead by reason and a gift for cooperation." He was effective in part because he understood his own weaknesses. He knew he was impatient, especially with the political "horse-trading" that usually preceded compromises among political leaders. Accordingly, he found aides who could work with senators and congressmen and other politicians, leaving him free to do what he did best. He left much of this kind of work to Joseph Tumulty, his private secretary. Tumulty, who had served in Wilson's New Jersey gubernatorial administration, knew his way around politicians and newspaper writers.

Above all, Wilson relied on the help of Colonel Edward M. House, a wealthy Texan who had become Wilson's friend and adviser in 1911. House was liberal, sophisticated, and politically astute. Wilson, who once called House "my second personality," deeply valued his friend's counsel about important political matters, such as the selection of cabinet members. "Talking to him," said the president, "is like talking to myself." The newspapers referred to Colonel House as the "assistant president" or the "silent partner."

House held no official position, but he was recognized everywhere as the president's personal representative. He and Tumulty and a small corps of other aides took care of the day-to-day chores of patronage (the distribution of jobs to reward political services), negotiation, and public relations.

As Wilson grew into the presidency, he sharpened his political skills. Elected at a time when the public supported reform, he quickly constructed an agenda for progressive legislative action. If one of his reforms stalled in Congress, he would generate pressure on the lawmakers to act by calling public attention to the delay. He also took advantage of Democratic majorities in the House and the Senate, insisting on their wholehearted support for the first Democratic president in 16 years.

With the exception of George Washington, Wilson guided more important laws through Congress than any of his predecessors. He first took aim at a traditional Democratic target, the high protective tariff.

Tariffs are taxes imposed by the government on imported goods. A "protective" tariff is one that makes an imported product cost as much as, or more than, similar products manufactured by the importing country. Those who favor such tariffs as-

Armed troopers encircle striking textile workers in Lawrence, Massachusetts, in 1912. Working conditions in New England's textile mills were wretched, and the pay was worse: men received a maximum of $10 for a 54-hour week. Because law enforcement officals were often in the employ of the mill owners, strikes were met with brutal force.

sert that they benefit the economy by protecting domestic producers from unfair competition. Tariffs, of course, also provide government revenue.

Those who oppose—as Wilson did—protective tariffs claim that in the long run they are dangerous to the economy. This group asserts that if foreign countries are prevented from selling their goods freely in the U.S. market, they will eventually run out of money with which to buy American goods. Thus, they say, protective tariffs hurt rather than help the economy.

Wilson persuaded, cajoled, and politicked furiously for the tariff-reduction legislation he wanted. Congress finally produced a law calling for the sharpest tariff decrease since the Civil War. To offset the resulting decline in revenue, the law contained another important progressive reform. This provision, which produced anguished howls from the nation's wealthy, imposed a federal tax on all incomes over $3,000.

Wilson next addressed the complex issue of banking reform. The nation's banking and currency system was outdated, unmanageable, and chaotic. Almost everyone — bankers, businessmen, con-

PRESIDENT WILSON SAYS:
"This is the time to support Woman Suffrage."

THE BETTMANN ARCHIVE

sumers, conservatives, progressives — agreed that it needed to be changed. There was, however, little agreement on how to do the job.

Wilson favored the establishment of a Federal Reserve Board, to be composed of presidentially appointed financial experts. The board would set national interest rates and manage a network of 12 big banks across the country. These institutions, which would issue currency, would in turn work with local banks.

Such a system would strike a heavy blow at the nation's staggeringly rich private bankers; predictably, this powerful group violently attacked Wilson and his scheme. Congress, its members concerned about the bankers' fury, dragged its feet. Christmas approached, but Wilson would not be moved. He forbade the legislators to go home for the holidays until they gave him the banking bill.

Finally, as Americans were trimming their trees and wrapping their gifts, the president got his Christmas present. On December 23, 1913, he signed the Federal Reserve Act.

Some historians call this landmark act the most important legislation produced by Wilson's administration. It created modern American currency (the Federal Reserve notes we use today) and provided

Demonstrating for their right to vote, women parade in New York City in 1916. The socially conservative Wilson was initially only lukewarm about women's suffrage (voting rights). In 1918, however, he finally announced his support for a constitutional amendment giving women the vote; it was ratified in August 1920.

NATIONAL ARCHIVES

General Francisco ("Pancho") Villa (center), leader of a guerrilla force trying to overthrow Mexico's civilian government, meets with fellow rebel officers in 1915. When Villa's forces began to raid American border towns and kill American citizens in 1916, Wilson sent U.S. troops into Mexico on a "punitive expedition" against the rebel leader.

the legal basis for an effective national banking system. It also protected the public interest by establishing the principle of government regulation of the banking system. Even the staunchly Republican *New York Tribune* called Wilson's shepherding of the Federal Reserve Act through Congress a "great exhibition of leadership."

The final major item on the agenda of the "New Freedom" was the reform of big business. This would involve the enactment of antitrust laws. A "trust" was a complicated arrangement that involved exchanges of stock among large companies. The term, however, had come to mean any secret partnership among competing industries. Such partnerships, which had become increasingly common toward the end of the 19th century, worked against the public by fixing prices, restraining competition, and dividing markets among the giant corporations. The trusts, by setting wages and forbidding strikes, also controlled and exploited millions of the nation's workers.

In his campaign for the presidency, Wilson had promised to work for new and effective laws to reduce the awesome power of the trusts. Now he began to implement that promise. In January 1914 he addressed a joint session of Congress, asking the legislators to turn their efforts toward anti-trust legislation.

Under the President's constant prodding, Congress produced two historic measures that dealt with business and labor. The first, which was passed in September 1914, established the Federal Trade Commission. This body was authorized to order companies to "cease and desist" from engaging in unfair competition. If a company failed to comply with the commission's order, it could be brought to court and forced to change its ways.

A month later, Congress passed the second anti-trust law. This was the Clayton Act, which outlawed a number of widely practiced business tactics. Now it was illegal for a group of companies to fix their prices in order to drive another company out of business. It was illegal for a manufacturer to refuse to sell to a dealer who also carried a competitor's products, and it was illegal for businesses to buy controlling stock in their competitors' companies.

The Clayton Act also supplied the labor movement with teeth. It said industry could no longer maintain power over unions by treating them as "unlawful combinations" or "conspiracies in restraint of trade." The act also legalized labor's major weapons —strikes, boycotts, and picket lines.

By the end of his first term, Wilson had much to be proud of on the domestic front. He had kept Congress in continuous session for a year and a half — something no president had ever done — and he had honored all his inaugural day promises.

Mexican and American soldiers prepare to search for Pancho Villa in 1917. Relations between the two nations were uneasy: fearing a U.S. invasion, Mexico was reluctant to allow American troops free rein in their pursuit of Villa; the Americans in turn were angered by Mexico's obstruction of their efforts to capture him.

His administration had produced major legislation on tariffs, banks, business, and labor. It had also been responsible for laws that restricted child labor, promoted the welfare of seamen, established compensation for injured workmen, and created a credit system for farmers. Wilson had made the "New Freedom" a reality. Interestingly, much of his reform legislation had originally been proposed by Theodore Roosevelt and rejected as too "radical" by Wilson.

The America of 1914 was not without foreign or domestic problems. There had been squabbles with Great Britain about the U.S.-owned Panama Canal, and diplomatic brushfires in Central America. The United States and Mexico had been on the verge of all-out war. At home, there were racial tensions and heated disputes between liberals and conservatives, between farmers and bankers, between industry and labor. Women were demanding the vote and church groups were appealing for the prohibition of liquor.

Nevertheless, the nation was at peace. The Wilson administration had made great progress toward improving society. Americans, secure between their protective oceans, were aware of people and events in other parts of the world, but they were not par-

U.S. General John J. ("Black Jack") Pershing leads his cavalry into Mexico in pursuit of Pancho Villa. The guerrilla chief escaped, but the Mexican government, regarding Pershing's raid as an invasion, mobilized its own army to fight the Americans. Full-scale war with Mexico was averted when the United States entered the conflict in Europe, and Wilson withdrew Pershing's troops.

[American Cartoon]

"What Will You Give for Her?"

—From The New York World.

A 1914 *New York World* cartoon reflects the attitude of many Americans about the plight of "poor little Belgium," as that unfortunate country was known. Despite Wilson's plea for "impartial thought," neither he nor millions of his countrymen were truly neutral about the brutal conflict raging in Europe.

ticularly interested in them. They were interested in progress, prosperity, the future. A feeling of safety and optimism prevailed. Then everything changed.

On June 28, 1914, a young Serbian terrorist assassinated Archduke Franz Ferdinand, heir to the throne of Austria-Hungary. To most Americans, the death of an obscure nobleman in a far-off country at first meant little. But that death would spark an inferno whose flames would soon engulf Europe. Its deadly fire would radiate outward, eventually searing most of the world, including America. The world would never be the same again.

By August all the great powers of Europe were at war. On one side were the Central Powers: Germany, Austria-Hungary, and Turkey; on the other were the Allies: Great Britain, France, and Russia. Both sides, eager for U.S. support, organized propaganda campaigns aimed at enlisting American sympathy.

German artillerymen shell French troops in Champagne, France. Most American military men expected the mighty German army to make short work of the French, but they underestimated the Gallic fighting spirit. France suffered terrible losses, but it responded valiantly to the battle cry first heard in 1916 at Verdun: "They shall not pass!"

Wilson wanted no part of this war. He wanted the United States to remain neutral, and he was deeply disturbed by the possibility that many Americans would identify with the countries from which they or their ancestors had emigrated. On August 4, 1914, he issued a proclamation of American neutrality. In a message to the Senate two weeks later he said, "The United States must be neutral in fact as well as in name. . . . We must be impartial in thought as well as in action, must put a curb upon our sentiments."

Remaining "impartial in thought," of course, was impossible, for Wilson as well as for other Americans. Wilson's sentiments, family background, and cultural associations all inclined him to view Great Britain as the center of culture and civilization. He viewed Britain's enemy, Germany, as the representative of aggressive militarism. Wilson's personal inclinations were strengthened by the course of events, particularly Germany's brutal invasion of neutral Belgium.

Wilson's sympathies with England were not simply prejudicial, nor did they rest solely on principle. Extremely powerful American investors such as J. P. Morgan had a great deal riding on the Allied war interests; England had been a lucrative market for American goods and for war loans at high interest rates. In 1915 Wilson lifted a then existing ban on private bank loans to the Allies, thereby furthering this connection between American finance and the British war effort, as well as casting doubt on the notion of American neutrality.

Millions of Americans felt as their president did about the justice of the Allied cause. Millions of others did not. Most of those who favored the Allies were in the South and on the East and West Coasts; many midwesterners, especially those with German backgrounds, viewed Germany and the Central Powers with some degree of sympathy. The bulk of the nation's citizens, however, favored neither side, insisting that foreign wars were no business of the United States. The conviction that a nation should remain uninvolved with affairs in other parts of the world is called isolationism. Wilson struggled constantly between isolationist sentiments and the necessity for American involvement in world affairs.

The outbreak of World War I coincided with a personal tragedy for Woodrow Wilson. Ellen Wilson had contracted tuberculosis, a disease for which no cure was known. On August 6, 1914, she died, leaving her husband almost paralyzed with grief. He sat beside her body for two days. In a letter to a friend he said, "God has stricken me almost beyond what I can bear."

Wilson had depended on Ellen for both love and counsel for 29 years, and now he was alone. His three grown daughters had left home, two of them to get married, one to pursue a singing career in New York City. The only woman left in his household was his cousin, Helen Woodrow Bones, who two months after Ellen's death made a sad observation: "No one can offer Cousin Woodrow any word of comfort, for there is no comfort."

The example of America must be an example, not of peace because it will not fight, but of peace because peace is the healing and elevating influence of the world, and strife is not. There is such a thing as a man being too proud to fight. There is such a thing as a man being so right that he does not need to convince others by force that he is right.
—WOODROW WILSON

A German soldier lies dead in a trench in France. Both sides constructed a line of trenches along the western front, which followed the border between Belgium and France. The trench-war casualties were appalling, but for almost four years neither side won or lost more than a few miles at a time.

Wilson took up golf and motoring in an effort to fill the time when he was not working; he also drew closer to his friend Edward House. Still, the president was inconsolable. His friends tried desperately to draw him away from his intense mourning. Eight months after Ellen's death, they introduced him to a beautiful and sympathetic widow named Edith Bolling Galt.

Forty-two years old, Edith Galt was a descendant of the Indian princess Pocahontas. She had grown up in a small town in Virginia, later marrying the owner of a prosperous Washington, D.C., jewelry store. After her husband's death, she had successfully operated the business. She smiled easily, was soft-spoken, gray-eyed, and dark-haired. "A fine figure of a woman," wrote Colonel Edmund Starling of the White House Secret Service, although "somewhat plump by modern American standards."

Wilson was 58 years old in the spring of 1915. Lean, five feet, eleven inches tall, he had gray-blue eyes and hair lightly touched with gray. Because of a minor stroke suffered in 1906, he had a slight defect in his left eye, and he wore pince-nez eyeglasses, which were in style at the time. Now, barely recovered from his wife's death, deeply involved in complex political and international issues, Woodrow Wilson fell deeply, boyishly in love.

Galt visited the White House often, and life there changed dramatically. Wilson installed a special telephone line between his room and Galt's home; he spent hours composing letters to her, and sent her orchids every day. According to White House usher Ike Hoover, "The president was simply obsessed. He put aside practically everything, dealing only with the most important matters of state."

Wilson and Galt took frequent drives together in his car, a Pierce Arrow with presidential seals on the doors and a top that could be removed in the summer. Washingtonians grew accustomed to the sight of the vehicle as, preceded by one Secret Service car and followed by another, it carried the starry-eyed couple through the city's streets.

On May 7, 1915, the British liner *Lusitania* was sunk by German submarines, precipitating a nationwide uproar in the United States. Two days later, Wilson wrote Galt, "I *need* you. I need you as a boy needs his sweetheart and a strong man his helpmate and heart's comrade." A month after that, still busy with the *Lusitania* crisis, he wrote, "If ever again I have to be with you for an hour and a half with only two stolen glances to express my all but irresistible desire to take you in my arms and smother you with kisses, I am sure I shall crack an artery!" Wilson and Galt were married on December 18, 1915.

Newspaper writers sometimes described Wilson as a cold, aloof man; clearly this applied only to his public personality. His reputation for remoteness arose from his fiercely protective attitude toward his own and his family's privacy. He refused to supply eager newspaper reporters with any details about his life and personality, even details that might have increased his popularity among the voters. Consequently, many of his attractive traits — his talent for mimicry, his love of limericks, his thorough knowledge of baseball—were unknown to the public.

Still, Wilson was ambivalent about his image. He once complained about being regarded as "a cold and removed person who has a thinking machine inside" and he also expressed regret that he was not known by a nickname; no one on record ever called him "Woody."

> *I want the people to love me, but I suppose they never will.*
> —WOODROW WILSON

Many U.S. newspapers carried this romantic collage of Wilson and Edith Galt, who were married in December 1915. Edith Galt Wilson, who outlived her husband by 37 years, maintained a lifelong dedication to the League of Nations and the other causes in which her husband had believed.

5

A Nation at War

The brutal realities of World War I, though geographically remote, were coming into sharper focus for the United States. Wilson, of course, followed the day-to-day events of the war but, ever the historian, he also considered its beginnings and its aftermath. "A hundred years from now," he said to a journalist in 1916, "it will not be the bloody details that the world will think of in this war: it will be the causes behind it, the readjustments which it will force."

In the same year, he wrote in his journal, "War, before this one, used to be a sort of national excursion, a necessary holiday. . . . But can this vast, gruesome contest of systematized destruction which we have witnessed for the last two years be pictured in that light? Deprived of glory, war loses its charm." Determined to avoid what he called Europe's "mechanical game of slaughter," the president rigorously pursued neutrality from 1914 to 1917. In the end, though, not even Woodrow Wilson could keep the United States out of World War I.

As the war increased in fury, Wilson's dealings with the great powers of Europe grew more and more complex. He was handicapped in these ne-

War is a series of catastrophes that result in victory.
—GEORGES CLEMENCEAU
French premier

The Democrats' 1916 campaign slogan was "He kept us out of war!" Wilson was sincerely committed to American neutrality, but he never promised to maintain it under all circumstances. By 1917 he believed the United States had no choice but to declare war on Germany.

gotiations by several factors. He was facing nations that had been established for centuries, nations that had picked their way through countless wars, and that were highly experienced in intricate diplomacy and espionage. The United States was a young country, unprepared for international diplomatic strategy. Its State Department, all-important in such matters, was still a small agency, staffed largely by amateurs. It had no organized system for collecting military or economic intelligence about other countries.

Wilson's effectiveness was further limited by the quality of his advisers. William Jennings Bryan had served as secretary of state from the beginning of Wilson's presidency. Bryan knew almost nothing about foreign affairs when he entered the government, and there is little evidence that he learned much in office.

The secretary of state strenuously objected to the way Wilson handled the aftermath of the *Lusitania* tragedy. In a series of sharply worded protests, Wilson condemned the German assault on the British ship. Germany replied that all the waters around the British Isles were a "war zone," and that it had the right to sink any ship that entered that zone carrying supplies for the Allies. The German argument was that any ship carrying supplies and munitions could not be considered neutral, and that the *Lusitania* was such a ship. Bryan thought Germany was within its rights.

When Wilson sternly rejected the legality of the "war zone" concept, Bryan resigned, claiming that the president's attitude toward Germany put the United States at risk of war. He was succeeded by diplomat Robert Lansing. According to many historians, Lansing's appointment was one of the worst mistakes Wilson ever made. Before Wilson finally fired him in 1920, Lansing had repeatedly weakened Wilson's authority by following his own course rather than the president's.

Even the loyal Colonel House began to disagree with Wilson's views on war and peace, eventually becoming more of a liability than an asset. Lansing and House were passionately pro-British; their ap-

AP/WIDE WORLD PHOTOS

William Jennings Bryan, Wilson's first secretary of state, was a deeply committed pacifist who opposed war under any conditions. He resigned in protest of Wilson's stern note to Germany about the *Lusitania*; once America was committed to fight, however, he urged support of Wilson's war policy.

proach to the international situation worked at cross purposes with Wilson's efforts to preserve U.S. neutrality.

Keeping America out of the war proved to be an extremely difficult — and eventually impossible — job. Wilson's greatest problems concerned shipping. Even the British, with whose cause the Americans clearly sympathized, behaved in an increasingly belligerent manner toward U.S. merchant vessels. The British, who had the strongest navy in the world, had thrown a blockade around Germany. They stopped and searched all neutral ships; if the ships' cargoes were bound for Germany, they were seized.

The British paid for the goods they confiscated, but the United States regarded the interference in its sea trade as a violation of both freedom of the seas and neutral rights. Wilson's protests, however, were in vain. The British maintained that they were fighting for their very survival, and that they could not afford to abide by such old-fashioned concepts as "freedom of the seas."

By 1916 Wilson was, as he put it, "about at the end of my patience with Great Britain and the Allies." He never considered retaliating, however. When he was urged by some members of his cabinet to place an embargo on exports to Britain, he refused. Making no mention of any economic considerations, Wilson said, "Gentlemen, the Allies are standing with their backs against the wall fighting wild beasts."

The United States's problems with Britain were serious, but its troubles with Germany were calamitous. Wilson's protests after the sinking of the *Lusitania* had produced a German promise that it would modify its submarine warfare against neutral shipping. In March 1916, however, Germany torpedoed the *Sussex*, a French channel steamer. Eighty civilians, some of them Americans, were killed. By this time, more than 200 American lives had been lost in German submarine attacks.

Wilson pointed out that while the United States was angry about British naval actions against American ships, these actions involved only property; Germany's tactics, he said, ignored "the fundamental rights of humanity." After the *Sussex* incident, he told Germany that unless these attacks ceased immediately, "the United States can have no choice but to sever diplomatic relations." The die was cast.

Inevitably, the issues of war and peace played a large role in the 1916 presidential election. Campaigning for reelection, Wilson concentrated on two things: his achievement of progressive reform at home and his success in keeping the nation out of war. He was perfectly confident about the first claim, but privately, he was not at all sure that he had entirely accomplished the second and he held little hope for future neutrality. "I can't keep the country out of war," he told Navy Secretary Josephus Daniels. "They talk of me as though I were a god. Any little German lieutenant can put us into the war at any time by some calculated outrage."

Wilson's Republican opponent was Charles Evans Hughes, an associate Supreme Court justice. Hughes attacked Wilson's domestic record as ineffective, and accused the president of pursuing an overcautious and unimaginative foreign policy. With the evidence of Wilson's reforms fresh in their minds, many Americans were unimpressed with Hughes's criticisms of Wilson's domestic record. And, still basically neutral, they were not so sure that caution in foreign affairs was a bad idea.

Nevertheless, the bearded judge appealed to many Americans, including the millions who loved Theodore Roosevelt. The popular "Teddy" gave his full backing to Hughes, who represented, he said, "clean-cut, straight-out Americanism." It was a very close election — the closest, in fact, since 1876, when Rutherford B. Hayes narrowly defeated Samuel J. Tilden. Hughes received 46 percent of the vote; Wilson drew a winning 49.3 percent. He had four more years to reform the world.

> *I am, I must admit, about at the end of my patience with Great Britain and the Allies. This black list business is the last straw. . . . Can we any longer endure their intolerable course?*
> —WOODROW WILSON
> 1916

Wilson's appointment of Robert Lansing as Bryan's successor in the State Department has been called one of Wilson's worst mistakes. Lansing was passionately pro-British; his efforts to make concessions to England after the war severely undercut Wilson's own plans for peace.

Wilson now mounted a major effort to bring about peace. Appealing to both sides, he called for an immediate end to the fighting and a return to the conditions that existed before the war. He outlined his plan for "peace without victory" on January 22, 1917: "Victory would mean peace forced upon the loser, a victor's terms imposed upon the vanquished." Such a victory, he said, would leave a "bitter memory upon which terms of peace would rest, not permanently, but only as upon quicksand. Only a peace between equals can last." The peace initiative failed. The Allies bitterly resented Wilson's effort; encouraged by Lansing and House, they had expected American policy to favor their own harsh terms for ending the war. And when the Germans learned of the peace initiative, they decided that the

Draped in an American flag, the coffin of a passenger killed on the *Lusitania* is carried through the streets of New York. Although the sinking of the British liner predated America's entry into the war by almost two years, it helped turn popular opinion against Germany.

A police officer fingerprints a German-born resident of New York City. Once the United States had entered into war against Germany, anti-German sentiment reached almost hysterical proportions. Anyone whose birth, accent, or philosophy even suggested a connection with Germany was considered a potential saboteur.

moment had arrived to make an all-out strike for victory.

On January 31, 1917, Germany announced that it would begin to wage unrestricted submarine warfare the following day. Germany would sink without warning every vessel, neutral as well as Allied, passenger liner as well as merchant ship, that approached Britain or the coast of France. Joe Tumulty brought the news to Wilson. "This means war," said the ashen-faced president. "The break that we have tried to prevent now seems inevitable."

Still he hesitated, hoping for some event that would make an American declaration of war unnecessary. Instead, two subsequent events destroyed all hope of continued neutrality.

The first was the Zimmermann Telegram. This was an astonishing message from German Foreign Secretary Arthur Zimmermann to the German minister in Mexico. Intercepted and decoded by British intelligence, the cable instructed the minister to make a deal: if Wilson declared war against Germany, Mexico was to attack the United States; in return, Germany would help Mexico recover its "lost territory in New Mexico, Texas, and Arizona." The Zimmermann Telegram, which Wilson made public on March 1, produced howls of outrage from the American press.

Charles Evan Hughes, the Republican candidate for president in 1916, resigned from the Supreme Court to run against Wilson. He appeared to have won the election until the very last moment; when the final ballots — California's — were all counted, they tipped the election in favor of Wilson.

The next event that pushed the United States toward war occurred in one of the Allied nations. In mid-March the world learned that Russia's autocratic tsar, Nicholas II, had been overthrown in a revolution. He had been replaced by a provisional government representing the common people. This meant that the Allied powers no longer included a repressive monarchy; the war could now be seen as a battle between tyrannies and democracies, a conflict in which Americans could engage with clear consciences.

American fury toward Germany was seething. It came to a full boil with the news, on March 18, that three more U.S. ships had been torpedoed by German submarines. Another two went down soon afterward, adding to the already heavy American death toll.

Public opinion demanded strong action. On April 6, 1917, the United States went to war and Wilson became the leader of the mighty effort to defeat the Central Powers. He pledged to use "force, force to the utmost, force without stint or limit," and dropped all talk of "peace without victory," aiming at victory pure and simple.

Thousands of young American men had volunteered to join the army even before the nation entered the war. But it was estimated that several million men were needed, and, during the six weeks following the declaration of war, only 75,000 men enlisted. In total there were only 375,000 men in uniform; the United States was far from ready to "make the world safe for democracy." "The army in April 1917," writes historian Robert H. Ferrell, "was a home for old soldiers, a quiet, sleepy place where they killed time until they began drawing their pensions."

Wilhelm II, Germany's kaiser (emperor), confers with his principal lieutenants, General Paul von Hindenburg (at left), chief of the German general staff, and Erich Ludendorff (at right), quartermaster general of the German army. Ludendorff was largely responsible for Germany's program of unrestricted submarine warfare.

On May 18, 1917, Congress passed the Selective Service Act, which required all men between the ages of 21 and 30 to register for military service. By June 5, 9.6 million men had registered; of these, 2.2 million were drafted into the army. By the end of the war, America had more than 4 million men in uniform.

But soldiers were of no use in the United States; somehow, the men and their equipment had to be transported to Europe. Their only route lay across an ocean alive with murderous German submarines, or U-boats. ("U-boat" is an abbreviation of the German *Unterseeboot*, which means "undersea boat.") One-fourth of the large ships that left British ports never returned; by the war's end, the U-boats had sunk 5,700 Allied vessels. Most Allied merchant ships had sailed alone, their captains believing that a single ship could most efficiently dodge submarines. The growing number of submarine "kills," however, proved this theory wrong; a lone vessel was easy prey.

In 1917 the British and American navies adopted the convoy system. A convoy consisted of a fleet of troop transports and supply ships, surrounded by an escort of antisubmarine destroyers. Convoys proved remarkably effective; after they were intro-

Curious Britishers inspect a German submarine, or U-boat, as it lies stranded off England's coast after the war. Germany's deadly fleet of U-boats wreaked immense destruction on Allied shipping; their attacks on U.S. merchant ships eventually pushed America into the war.

THE BETTMANN ARCHIVE

Bolshevik soldiers stand guard in 1917 over an important prisoner: Nicholas II, Russia's deposed tsar. After Russia's revolutionary government signed a separate peace with Germany in 1918, Nicholas and his family were murdered.

duced, not a single American troopship was sunk, although two British ships carrying American soldiers went down with a loss of 222 lives. Later in the war, the U.S. Navy used airplanes to spot submarines and warn Allied ships of their presence.

The American Expeditionary Force (or AEF, as it was popularly known) was under the command of General John J. "Black Jack" Pershing. Led by Pershing, the first American soldiers landed in France in June 1917. Americans saw the soldiers off with brass bands and festive parades. The nation rang with patriotic and sentimental songs: "Over There," "Yankee Doodle Dandy," "The Rose of No Man's Land." Almost everyone seemed to believe that these men were off to fight a "great crusade" that would create a better world. "The eyes of all the

Blindfolded, Secretary of War Newton D. Baker draws the number of a man who will be drafted into the army. The 1917 Selective Service Act required all men between the ages of 21 and 30 to register. The order in which they were called up was determined by lotteries like this one.

world will be upon you," said an emotional Wilson to a departing shipload of troops, "because you are in some special sense the soldiers of freedom."

At the end of 1917 there were 180,000 U.S. troops in France. Faced with severe military losses, the Allies pleaded for more volunteers, and in 1918, America began what was called the "race to France." By the summer of 1918, 300,000 American soldiers had arrived in France; by the end of the war, the number had topped 2 million.

The rush to mobilize the AEF had not allowed enough time to train the American soldiers properly. They were quick, however, to master the deadly arts of war, and they soon earned the respect of the seasoned Allied armies. The Americans' first important engagement came in June 1918. The German army, intent on capturing Paris, had advanced to Château-Thierry, a village less than 50 miles from the French capital. Chaos prevailed as the Germans attacked French forces in Belleau Wood, a small forest nearby.

As the French were retreating in confusion, thousands of "Black Jack" Pershing's Marines swept into the woods. Future British Prime Minister Winston Churchill said the Americans affected the beleaguered French like a "transfusion of blood." The Marines won the battle of Belleau Wood, but at an appalling cost: 5,183 of the 8,000 Marines who fought there were killed or wounded.

In September 1918 an American army of half a million men joined French forces in attacking St. Mihiel salient, a German position on the Meuse River, south of Verdun. The Americans defeated the Germans after two days of savage fighting. They captured 16,000 Germans and 400 guns, but more than 7,000 Americans were killed or wounded.

From September to November, Pershing's troops, now numbering almost 1 million men, battled the Germans in the Argonne Woods and the marshes of the Meuse River, near the Belgian border. Known as the Meuse-Argonne offensive, this was the biggest and fiercest campaign of the war, inflicting more than 120,000 American casualties. The French and American forces captured 48,800 prisoners and 1,424 guns. The Meuse-Argonne offensive, which was coordinated with an Allied drive against the Central Powers all across Europe, put the end of the war in sight.

The Americans' hard-won victories against the Germans owed a great deal to the speed with which the United States, under Wilson's leadership, mobilized for war. From April 1917 until the war ended in November 1918, the nation suspended its normal operating procedures. Under special powers granted to him by Congress, Wilson created a powerful new government body, the Council of National Defense. The council, made up of cabinet members and civilians, directed the operations of the six sub-agencies that, in effect, ran the country during the war.

The most powerful of these agencies was the War Industries Board, which had virtually dictatorial powers over American business, controlling both

Taking cover in a devastated French forest, American soldiers open fire against the German army. By 1918 the grim and seemingly endless war had transformed much of the French countryside into a ghostly wasteland, punctuated only by lines of trenches, shattered trees, and rows of graves.

production and prices. During the war, America's industries supplied war materials for British and French, as well as U.S., troops. Military engagement did wonders for the American economy; industrial production of war materials meant more jobs for workers and even greater profits for wealthy industrialists and financiers. Prior to this engagement the United States had begun to experience a recession, but as the American war industry grew, the economy was revived. As one historian has said, "America became bound up with the Allies in a fateful union of war and prosperity."

Another agency was the Food Administration, headed by Herbert Hoover, a capable and resourceful mining engineer who would serve as president of the United States from 1929 to 1933. Hoover's agency was responsible for producing and distributing food for both the civilian and military popu-

Swashbuckling movie hero Douglas Fairbanks leads a Liberty Bond rally in New York City. Fairbanks and other celebrities helped make the bond drives a runaway success: eager Americans bought $18.5 billion worth of the interest-paying bonds, which were used to help finance the war.

lations, as well as for much of war-torn Europe. Under his leadership, Americans reformed their traditionally wasteful ways and accepted such novel practices as "meatless Tuesdays." The result was a tripling of the amount of food available for shipment overseas.

Other wartime agencies included the Fuel Administration, which managed the distribution of coal and oil, and the Railroad Administration, which coordinated the operations of the nation's private rail systems. In charge of railroads was William McAdoo, secretary of the Treasury and the husband of Wilson's youngest daughter, Eleanor.

From the first meeting of Congress in 1789 after the adoption of the U.S. Constitution until April 6, 1917, the total cost of running the government had

Mounted New York City policemen charge a rally sponsored by the Industrial Workers of the World. The IWW, a radical labor organization, militantly opposed the war. It was virtually destroyed by the government, which relentlessly prosecuted it under wartime sedition laws.

been $24 billion. Now, in only 18 months, the government would spend $35.5 billion to defeat the Germans and their allies. To pay for the war, Congress passed the War Revenues Act of 1917, which increased taxes on incomes and wartime profits.

The government also relied on income from the "Liberty Loan" project, another effort managed by William McAdoo. It was McAdoo's job to persuade the public to buy income-producing government certificates known as Liberty Bonds. He organized rallies and parades, distributed posters, and enlisted the help of such famous movie stars as Mary Pickford and Douglas Fairbanks. The drive was a great success; Americans snapped up every bond the government issued.

America's mobilization for war was impressive but was not without dissent. Antiwar demonstrations throughout the Midwest drew large crowds and even the mainstream newspapers continued references to the "unpopular" war. Wilson had earlier asked Americans to remain neutral in thought as well as action; now he expected them to support the war totally. As a result, American sentiments were mixed.

Socialist leader Eugene V. Debs addresses an antiwar rally in Canton, Ohio, in 1918. Debs's speech earned him a 10-year prison sentence under the 1917 Espionage Act. Still in jail in 1920, he ran for president and won almost 1 million votes, many cast by people who regarded the Espionage Act as unjust.

The U.S. War Department asked J. P. Morgan, Jr., son of the fabulously wealthy American financier, to help finance the war effort. He complied by arranging loans of more than $3 billion for Allied purchases, a patriotic move that proved extremely profitable for himself.

In 1917 Congress passed the Espionage Act; in 1918, the Sedition Act became law. These laws made it illegal — and punishable by fines up to $10,000 and 20-year prison terms — to interfere with the draft, hamper the sale of war bonds, or encourage disloyalty. Consequently, stiff penalties were imposed on people who dared to "utter, paint, write, or publish any disloyal, profane, scurrilous, or abusive language" about the government.

More than 1,500 Americans went to jail under the espionage and sedition laws. Among them were 450 conscientious objectors — men who refused to fight because of their religious or ethical beliefs. Eugene

V. Debs, the popular leader of the U.S. Socialist party, was sentenced to 10 years in jail for an anti-war speech; so was a woman whose crime consisted of writing, "I am for the people, and the government is for the profiteers."

Wilson's approval of the espionage and sedition laws startled and disappointed many of his strongest supporters. Most Americans, however, were strangely silent about these assaults on their civil liberties. They put up with them because they believed that the nation was crawling with traitors and German spies — a belief that sprang from the government's efforts to whip the nation into a patriotic frenzy. The national press tended to support the legislation. *The New York Times*, for instance, ran a 1917 editorial stating, "It is the duty of every good

U.S. soldiers herd a column of German prisoners, captured during the American assault on St. Mihiel on September 12, 1917, through a French village. The successful attack netted 16,000 German prisoners, but its cost was appalling: American forces suffered more than 7,000 casualties.

citizen to communicate to proper authorities any evidence of sedition that comes to his notice." Despite these laws, however, 65,000 men declared themselves conscientious objectors to the war.

Soon after the declaration of war, Congress had established the Committee on Public Information, which was actually a ministry of propaganda. The committee embarked on a campaign to make Americans hate Germans. The teaching of the German language was discontinued in schools; German music (including Beethoven's) was prohibited; books by German authors were removed from public libraries and sometimes even thrown into public bonfires. The wave of anti-German sentiment became so extreme — and ridiculous — that dachshunds were renamed "liberty pups" and sauerkraut was labeled "liberty cabbage."

Wilson believed that this war — perhaps more lacking in glory and more filled with horror than any previous conflict — at least served one good purpose. It would provide, he thought, a unique opportunity to prevent future wars.

He was determined to control the peace that would be made once the war ended. A generous peace, one that contained no seeds of future discord, might be possible. But it could never be achieved, Wilson felt, unless the Allies were prevented from grasping as much as possible from the enemy. He knew of secret pacts, such as the Treaty of London, by which Britain, France, Russia, and Italy had agreed to divide Germany and Austria-Hungary among themselves after the war. He had no intention of letting such behind-the-scenes manuevering sabotage the opportunity for an enduring worldwide peace.

On January 8, 1918 — 10 months before the war ended — Wilson made a historic speech before Congress. In it, he listed his outline for a peace plan. His proposal, known as the Fourteen Points, would be read and admired by people all over the world. First on Wilson's list of goals was "open covenants [treaties] of peace, openly arrived at." He wanted no part of secret diplomacy, no dirty little secrets between greedy nations.

The next objectives were freedom of the seas and

> *Mr. Wilson's name among the Allies is like that of the rich uncle, and they have accepted his manners out of respect for his means.*
> —*London Morning Post*, 1919

the removal of trade barriers. The fourth point — very important, in Wilson's mind — was disarmament. Wilson next listed the adjustment of colonial claims, insisting that the people who lived in countries ruled by other nations should have a say in their own fate. The next eight points dealt with the realignment of borders and the evacuation of occupying troops from conquered nations.

The last of Wilson's Fourteen Points was the one dearest to his heart: "A general association of nations must be formed under specific covenants for the purpose of affording mutual guarantees of political independence and territorial integrity to great and small states alike." He was proposing, in other words, a League of Nations, in which all countries, not just the powerful ones, would have a voice.

The war-weary people of the world responded enthusiastically to Wilson's words. Indeed, throughout the next two decades, collections of Wilson's speeches would be popular in such disparate places as Spain and China, and his portrait would hang in private homes, from mansions to hovels, all over Europe. He had become the leader of all those who hoped for a generous, liberal, permanent peace.

By the autumn of 1918 Germany's armies were in retreat, its navy close to mutiny, its civilians hungry, exhausted, and on the verge of revolt. In October, Germany sent a spokesman to talk to Wilson about peace. Germany, the spokesman said, would be willing to sign an armistice (truce) based on Wilson's Fourteen Points. Wilson was willing to talk, but he said Germany would have to replace the military leaders in its government with civilians before peace terms could be arranged with the Allies. Wilson was sure once Germany had a new government, the only thing needed would be the Allied governments' agreement to accept peace on the basis of the Fourteen Points. But the British and French refused to accept that basis.

Representing Wilson in Paris, Colonel House applied pressure on the Allies. He said that unless they accepted the Fourteen Points, the United States would have to begin peace talks alone. "That would amount," said French Premier Georges Clemenceau, "to a separate peace between the United States and the Central Powers." "It might," House replied. "My statement," Colonel House cabled Wilson, "had a very exciting effect on those present." Indeed, it led the next day to British and French acceptance of most of the Fourteen Points — excluding freedom of the seas—as a basis of peace.

The German government finally signed an armistice on November 11. By the time the killing stopped, more than 100,000 American lives had been lost. The overall toll, including soldiers and civilians of all the warring nations, had reached the staggering total of 10 million dead.

A French couple greet their American liberators in 1918. The "Yanks," young, idealistic, brave — and numerous — were warmly welcomed by the war-weary Europeans. "They were," recalled one French peasant, "so young and looked so innocent, and were so far from home."

6

The Peacemaker

Woodrow Wilson, the pacifist, had led his nation into war "to make the world safe for democracy." He justified America's participation in the war by pointing out that only as a fighting nation could the United States participate fully in the peace negotiations. When the war finally ended, Wilson turned to what he thought would be the rewarding job of forging an enduring peace.

Wilson passionately wanted his Fourteen Points implemented at the peace conference that followed the 1918 armistice. He wanted a treaty that would be fair to the fallen enemy as well as to the victors. He longed to be the architect of permanent peace in the world. But he handicapped himself at the outset of the peace negotiations by making a number of ill-advised decisions.

His first mistake was his choice of American representatives to the postwar peace conference in Paris. They included Secretary of State Lansing, at best a vacillating supporter of Wilson's policies, at worst a genuine stumbling block. Lansing's enthusiasm for Wilson's cherished fourteenth point — the League of Nations—was almost nonexistent.

> *Unless you get the united, concerted purpose and power of the great governments of the world behind the settlement, it will fall down like a house of cards.*
> —WOODROW WILSON
> on the importance of the
> League of Nations

Woodrow and Edith Wilson triumphantly enter Paris in December 1918, a month after the end of World War I. Quite possibly the most popular man in the world at this point, Wilson was confident that he could achieve a just and lasting peace.

Another negotiator was Colonel House. He was an able diplomat, but he was in a hurry to get the peace treaty settled. His strong pro-British feelings led him to push for more concessions to the British than Wilson wanted. Furthermore, Wilson's confidence in House had diminished, which reduced his usefulness as a spokesman for his chief. Some historians blame the breakdown in trust between the two men on Wilson's wife Edith, who was said to detest her husband's longtime confidant. Most of the other representatives were weak and relatively uninfluential.

Wilson also erred by failing to appoint any leading Republicans to the American team. This both offended a large percentage of American voters and lost crucial political support for Wilson's goals. More damaging still had been Wilson's appeal to voters in the fall's congressional elections; he had asked them to demonstrate their support of his policies by electing only Democrats.

Home at last, a shipload of cheering soldiers enters a New York harbor in 1919. More than 2 million American soldiers had gone to Europe, and 1.3 million of them saw action on the front lines. Many never returned; over 100,000 Americans were killed in the war.

Since many Republicans had firmly supported Wilson's wartime programs, and since they, too, were committed to obtaining a solid peace treaty, they bitterly resented Wilson's partisan appeal. The election produced a Republican majority in both houses of Congress. When Wilson went to Paris, it was with reduced prestige; he was seen as a leader who had lost the backing of his countrymen.

In spite of the problems Wilson had created for himself, he left for Paris in high spirits. He was brimming with optimism and ready to take on whatever opposition he might meet. "Tell me what's right," he said to reporters covering his December 1918 departure from New York, "and I'll fight for it!"

When Wilson arrived in Paris, he received a thunderous hero's welcome. Tens of thousands of Parisians lined the streets, cheering, crying, shouting "*Vive* [long live] Wilson!" It was the same story when Wilson and his wife toured England and Italy. The people of Europe greeted the American president as the savior of mankind.

The leaders of the Allied nations were another

Members of the American Peace Commission in France included (from left to right): Colonel Edward House, the president's long-time friend and adviser; Robert Lansing, Wilson's strongly pro-British secretary of state; Wilson; career diplomat Henry White; and General Tasker H. Bliss, the U.S. Army chief of staff.

matter. Here, Wilson was locking horns with cynical and sophisticated veterans of Europe's long-running political intrigues. The dominant voices at the conference were those of Wilson, Prime Minister David Lloyd George of Britain, Premier Georges Clemenceau of France, and Prime Minister Vittorio Orlando of Italy.

The other members of the "Big Four" regarded Wilson as naive, unrealistic, even self-righteous. Clemenceau, whose political toughness had earned him the nickname, "the Tiger of France," was particularly exasperated by his idealistic counterpart. "President Wilson and his Fourteen Points bore me," exclaimed the Tiger at one point. "Even God Almighty had only ten!"

Another sniper was Lloyd George. After the conference, he was asked how things had gone in Paris. "I think I did as well as might be expected," he replied, "seated between Jesus Christ [Wilson] and Napoleon Bonaparte [Clemenceau]."

The Peace Conference met at Versailles Palace, outside Paris, from January to June 1919. Attending along with the "Big Four" were delegates from the 32 other countries that had been officially at war with the Central Powers. Orlando, who quickly realized that Italy would not receive the Austro-Hun-

Visiting London, England, in early 1919, Wilson inspects a group of American soldiers who had been captured and imprisoned by the Germans. The former prisoners of war had been appointed by King George of England to serve as an honor guard at Buckingham Palace.

garian territories it had demanded, left the conference early; the core of the assemblage was now the "Big Three."

The American Peace Commission, as Wilson's delegation to the peace talks was called, consisted of 1,300 people. In all, 10,000 individuals came to Paris that winter, each claiming to have some important connection with the peace conference. American political columnist Walter Lippmann wrote, "The clamor converged on Paris, and all the winds of doctrine were set whirling around the conferees. Every dinner table . . . was a focus of intrigue and bluster and manufactured rumor."

Wilson and his colleagues battled on almost every major issue. Britain and France wanted Germany to pay for the whole war — a total of $120 billion. France wanted huge chunks of German territory, including the coal-rich Saar Basin. The newly created Polish state wanted to annex East Prussia. All the Allies except Wilson wanted the peace treaty to include a "war guilt" clause that forced Germany to admit full responsibility for starting the war — and thus full responsibility for paying for it.

Wilson, of course, wanted his Fourteen Points, which stood in opposition to almost everything the Allies demanded. Although he succeeded in taking the edge off the more extreme claims of the other countries, he was forced to make a number of concessions in order to obtain an agreement on the League of Nations. Among the concessions were the "war guilt" clause, and a $15 billion levy on Germany. Wilson also made a separate agreement with Clemenceau, promising that the United States would defend France against any future attack.

The Treaty of Versailles was completed and signed by Germany and the Allies in June 1919. It was, as Wilson noted, "a very severe settlement with Germany." Nevertheless, he added, "there is not anything in it that she did not earn." In spite of its harshness, the treaty — thanks to Wilson's conscientious efforts — was much closer to the Fourteen Points than anyone could reasonably have expected when the negotiations began. Belgian independence was restored, the French lands that had been

How can I talk to a fellow who thinks himself the first man in two thousand years to know anything about peace on earth?
—GEORGES CLEMENCEAU
French premier, on negotiating with Wilson

The "Big Four" meet at Versailles Palace, site of the Paris Peace Conference. Britain's Prime Minister David Lloyd George (left) addresses Prime Minister Vittorio Orlando of Italy, while Wilson (right) exchanges a word with Premier Georges Clemenceau of France.

annexed by Germany were returned to France, an independent Poland was created, and new democratic states, Czechoslavakia and Yugoslavia, were carved out of the old, autocratic Austro-Hungarian empire. Most important, at least to Wilson, an international organization was born.

Wilson could tolerate the treaty because he believed that, under the auspices of the League of Nations, the Allies would in time modify some of the agreement's harshest terms. In a message cabled to the American people, he said the treaty was "much more than a treaty of peace with Germany. It liberates great peoples. . . . It associates the free governments of the world in a permanent league . . . to maintain peace. . . . It makes international law a reality supported by imperative sanctions." Wilson expected the League to help the United States move away from its traditional isolationism and provincialism to take its rightful place as a leader in international affairs.

Ultimately, the question of the League acquired a terrible urgency for Wilson. If peace was not to be assured by United States participation in the League, what justification had there been for war, for the deaths of so many young Americans? In a speech he made soon after coming home, Wilson told of meeting women who had lost their sons in France. Many of these mothers, he reported, had shed tears as they said, "God bless you, Mr. President!" Why, asked Wilson rhetorically, "should they pray God to bless me? . . . I ordered their sons overseas. . . . Why should they weep upon my hand and call down the blessings of God upon me? Because they believe . . . and rightly believe, that their sons saved the liberty of the world." Now "the liberty of the world" depended upon the approval of the Versailles Treaty by the Senate of the United States.

On July 10 Wilson presented the treaty to the Senate for ratification, as required by the Constitution. Colonel House had suggested that the president approach the Senate in a conciliatory spirit, prepared to make some compromises. Wilson reportedly replied, "I have found that one can never get anything in this life that is worthwhile without fighting for it." To the Senate he said, "Dare we reject it and break the heart of the world?"

Confidently meeting with reporters after this speech, Wilson said he would oppose all modifications of the treaty. After all, 32 state legislatures had endorsed it, 33 governors said that they approved, and a poll by the magazine *Literary Digest* showed overwhelming support among the editors of newspapers and magazines.

But the treaty also had strong opposition. Many liberals and progressives considered it worthless because Wilson had failed to achieve all of the Fourteen Points. Some German-Americans and Italian-Amer-

> *There is only one power to put behind the liberation of mankind, and that is the power of mankind. It is the power of the united moral forces of the world, and in the Covenant of the League of Nations the moral forces of the world are mobilized.*
> —WOODROW WILSON

The Treaty of Versailles in his pocket, Wilson tips his top hat as he returns from Europe in June 1919. The president was exhausted, but he was still confident that Congress would approve the treaty, and with it, U.S. membership in the League of Nations.

icans felt it was too harsh on Germany and Italy, and some Irish-Americans denounced its failure to free Ireland from British control. Isolationists, traditionally a strong voice in American politics, feared that the treaty would involve the United States in the conflicts of other nations.

The Republicans, still angry about Wilson's call for an all-Democratic Congress in the 1918 election and about his failure to include any of their number on the Peace Commission, controlled the Senate. The chairman of the crucial Foreign Relations Committee was Henry Cabot Lodge of Massachusetts. An old friend of Theodore Roosevelt, Lodge personally disliked Wilson, whose idealism and concern for morality in international affairs he found both irritating and unrealistic. Lodge spearheaded the movement opposing the treaty's ratification.

Despite its antitreaty rumblings, however, the Senate was prepared to approve the treaty — and U.S. membership in the League of Nations — with certain reservations. But Wilson refused even to

Wilson greets a crowd in Columbus, Ohio, in September 1919. The midwestern city was one of dozens the president visited in hopes of gaining support for the League of Nations. Without the League, he repeatedly told audiences, "I can predict that within another generation there will be another world war."

consider modifying the document he had brought back from Paris. His hardline attitude galvanized the opposition, which, led by Lodge, began an all-out campaign to sink the treaty.

Wilson decided to make a nationwide tour, appealing directly to the voters on behalf of the treaty. He was exhausted after his marathon conferences in Paris and Washington, and his doctors urged him not to make the trip. But Wilson insisted on doing what he felt must be done. "You must remember," he said to his personal physician, Dr. Cary Grayson, "that I, as commander in chief, was responsible for sending our soldiers to Europe. In the crucial test in the trenches they did not turn back — and I cannot turn back now. I cannot put my personal safety, my health in the balance against my duty — I must go."

Wilson left Washington on September 3. In 22 days, he traveled 8,000 miles and delivered 32 major speeches. At every stop the president offered hope for the future. He talked about the children who greeted his train: "I look at them almost with tears in my eyes, because I feel my mission is to save them." He said that "if by any chance, we should not win this great fight for the League of Nations, it would be their death warrant."

If the League failed, Wilson told his audiences, he could "predict with absolute certainty that within another generation there will be another world war." He warned that new weapons would make future conflicts even bloodier. "What the Germans used were toys," he said, "compared to what would be used in the next war." He asked Americans to join him in accepting "the leadership of the world."

To an extent domestic opposition to the treaty had its roots in the postwar malaise that characterized the country during this period. The American public was deeply embittered and disillusioned by the devastating loss of life and the annihilation of human values the war had entailed. Literature written about these years in America, works like Ernest Hemingway's *A Farewell to Arms* and the John Dos Passos novel *1919*, portray a generation lost in the wake of the Great War.

After a speech in Pueblo, Colorado, on September 25, Wilson seemed unusually fatigued. He had, in fact, suffered a stroke, although the truth was covered up at the time. His doctor canceled the tour, and the train returned to Washington. On October 2, he suffered a second, massive stroke that paralyzed the left side of his face and body.

Wilson's collapse came at a critical time. Lodge had been busy during the president's absence, proposing a series of reservations to the treaty that he knew Wilson would never accept. The Senate scheduled a vote for November 19. By then, Wilson was able to sit up in bed, and his mind was as clear as ever. A senator from the pro-League faction called on him before the Senate vote; he said the treaty would not pass unless at least some of Lodge's reservations were accepted, and he urged Wilson to

The Supreme Court in 1917. Some government officials felt that if Wilson, virtually incapacitated by a stroke in September 1919, refused to step down, the issue should be brought before the Supreme Court; others believed that Congress should remove him. Wilson, however, recovered just enough of his health to govern until his term was over.

97

UPI/BETTMANN NEWSPHOTOS

The body of a young black man, the victim of a 1920 lynch mob, hangs from a tree in Paris, Kentucky. Racial violence had been an ongoing problem in the United States since the Civil War, but it reached a sickening crescendo in the years following World War I.

consider making some compromises. Ill or not, Wilson refused to budge. "Let Lodge compromise!" he thundered.

The Senate voted against Lodge's reservations. It also voted against ratifying the treaty without the reservations. (Only one Republican senator voted in favor of Wilson's version of the treaty.) If Wilson had accepted some of the reservations, he could have had a treaty. He chose not to give in, and as a result, wound up with nothing. "With his own sickly hands," observed historian Thomas A. Bailey, "Wilson slew his own brainchild."

In March 1920 the treaty was again introduced in the Senate, and once again Wilson instructed the Democrats to vote against any modifications. It failed to get the necessary two-thirds majority. This time, Wilson's dream of American participation in the League of Nations was dead once and for all.

With the treaty unsigned, the United States was still technically at war with Germany. In May Congress passed a joint resolution declaring the war over. Furious and disappointed at the failure of his treaty, Wilson vetoed the resolution. The war with Germany was not officially over until July 2, 1921, when legislation that ended it was signed by Wilson's successor.

Wilson's illness created an unprecedented situation. According to the Constitution, if a president was unable to "discharge the powers and duties" of his office, the presidency was to be taken over by the vice-president. But until the 25th Amendment to the Constitution was passed in 1967, there was no formal definition of presidential disability, and no indication of who should decide whether or not the president was disabled.

After Wilson's stroke, Secretary of State Lansing suggested to Edith Wilson and Wilson's secretary Joe Tumulty that the time had come for the president to step down in favor of his vice-president,

Ku Klux Klan members meet in Freeport, New York, in the 1920s. The modern Klan, founded in Georgia in 1915, was originally an instrument for keeping southern blacks "in their place." In the postwar years, however, the militantly racist organization spread its message across the United States.

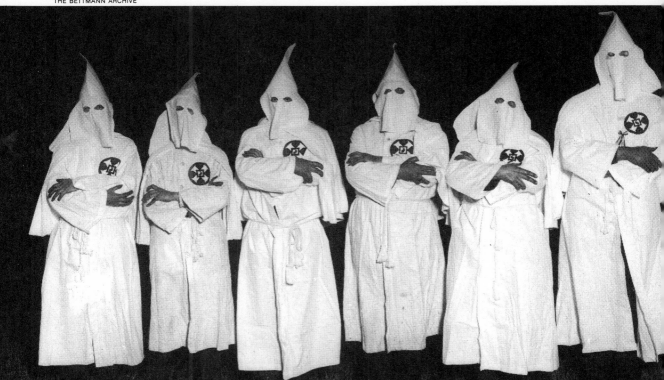

Thomas R. Marshall. Marshall was a likeable non-entity whose best-known words were, "What this country needs is a good five-cent cigar!" When he was asked how he would handle the job of president, Marshall groaned and said, "I can't even think about it." The president's wife and secretary flatly refused to consider Lansing's suggestion, and he dropped the idea.

By November Wilson's health had improved, although he found it difficult to concentrate on any subject for more than a few minutes at a time. While he was ill, Wilson saw no one but his wife and his doctor. Mrs. Wilson transmitted his orders and gave him documents to mark with his shaky signature.

Historians disagree on the subject of Wilson's condition during his last 17 months in office. Some biographers maintain that he was weak and easily tired but that he continued to govern actively. Others say he retained a limited grasp on his responsibilities. A third group maintains that he had become virtually incapacitated, and was president

Wilson's attorney general, A. Mitchell Palmer, was responsible for a series of quasi-legal raids on "anarchists" and "reds" that resulted in the arrest of thousands of innocent people. Mitchell finally lost credibility in May 1920 when, without evidence, he ordered 6,000 people arrested in New York City.

THE BETTMANN ARCHIVE

in name only. The record does show that several months after Wilson's massive stroke, Dr. Grayson said, "He is permanently ill physically, is gradually weakening mentally, and can't recover."

No medical bulletins were issued beyond Grayson's vague announcement of a "nervous breakdown." Wilson remained in seclusion for several months, communicating principally through his wife. It was she who handled all letters and documents sent to the president by his cabinet and Congress, and who conferred with the nation's invisible leader, emerging from the sickroom to report his orders. She guided Wilson's hand as he signed bills and strongly influenced decisions about presidential appointments. Some people said Edith Wilson had actually become the nation's president. One newspaper referred to "the Mrs. Wilson regency," and she herself spoke of "my stewardship."

The situation in the White House was viewed with alarm by some in Congress. Senator Albert Fall of New Mexico pounded on his desk and shouted, "We have a petticoat government! Mrs. Wilson is president!" He was apparently reassured about Wilson's mental health after a visit to the White House. He reported himself as saying, "We, Mr. President, have all been praying for you." Wilson looked at Fall with amusement. "Which way, Senator?" he asked.

Wilson's six months in Paris and his subsequent illness had left the nation without presidential leadership during the years immediately following the war. These were troubled times in the United States. Wilson's attorney general, an ambitious Pennsylvania politician named A. Mitchell Palmer, used the nation's fears of "anarchists" to launch a virulent and cruel campaign against the "Red Menace." Palmer, who saw such a course as a road to the White House, persuaded much of the country that bomb-throwing radicals and "Reds" lurked behind every lamppost. He organized a series of raids against alleged communists that resulted in a wave of mass hysteria and the illegal arrest of thousands of innocent people.

The early 1920s were also a time of racial tension. Many southern blacks had moved north during the

We have made partners of the women in this war; shall we admit them only to a partnership of suffering and sacrifice and toil and not to a partnership of privilege and right?
—WOODROW WILSON
campaigning for women's suffrage in 1918

war to work in defense plants. When such work diminished after the war, the blacks' presence was resented by white workers, and race riots became horrifyingly common. Violence against blacks spread, resulting in hundreds of deaths. Other minorities — Jews, Catholics, foreigners — also felt the bitter lash of intolerance; the 1920s would be one of the best of times for the Ku Klux Klan, an organization based on hatred of everyone it did not consider a "red-blooded American." Labor problems, too, troubled the nation. There were more major strikes and labor-management conflicts in 1919 than ever before in America's history.

It is not surprising, then, that many Americans lost confidence in Wilson. Although he was still a hero in the eyes of the rest of the world, by the fall of 1920 he had almost no supporters left in the United States. He briefly dreamed of becoming the Democratic presidential candidate in 1920, but the party passed him over in favor of a "dark horse," the little-known governor of Ohio, James M. Cox.

Cox, representing the party of Wilson, was doomed. Senator Lodge delivered the campaign theme of the Republican party in 1920: "Mr. Wilson and his dynasty, his heirs and assigns . . . must be driven from all control of the government and all influence in it." Warren G. Harding, the Republican candidate, was overwhelmingly elected president.

Wilson's last months in the White House were quiet. He was almost totally ignored by the nation, but in December 1920 the world's high opinion of him was confirmed: he was awarded the Nobel Peace prize. On March 4, 1921, he accompanied Harding to the Capitol for the new president's inauguration ceremony. The Wilsons then moved out of the limelight and into a new house in a quiet Washington residential area.

Unlike many ex-presidents, Wilson did not assume the role of elder statesman or spokesman for his party. He made almost no public statements after he left office. One of his rare appearances came on November 11, 1923, the fifth anniversary of the armistice that ended World War I. By now he was mortally ill, but he made it clear that he had never

The IWW's aim was the establishment of immense, worker-controlled unions that would seize control of industry and destroy capitalism. The organization was all but wiped out by government harrassment during World War I, but its posters continued to be displayed by redbaiters in the 1920s.

doubted his own policies. "I am not one of those that have the least anxiety about the triumph of the principles I have stood for," he told a crowd of well-wishers outside his Washington home. "That we shall prevail is as sure as that God reigns."

Less than three months later, weeping admirers gathered outside Wilson's Washington home, praying as they waited for what could only be sad news. Inside, Wilson spoke to his doctor. "The machinery is worn out," he said. "I am ready." Woodrow Wilson, 67 years old, died on February 3, 1924.

Wilson's funeral procession. Although the 28th president's reputation had shrunk by the time of his death in 1924, later appraisals of his career have been high. He was, wrote historian Samuel Eliot Morrison, "a great leader because he sensed the aspirations of plain people and expressed them in phrases that rang like a great bronze bell."

7

Wilson in Perspective

Woodrow Wilson was a complex man. In his character were both extraordinary strengths and glaring limitations. His impact on the world was controversial as well as powerful, inspiring contradictory assessments of his abilities and intentions.

A few months after the Paris negotiations, British economist John Maynard Keynes published a highly influential, best-selling book, *The Economic Consequences of the Peace*. In it Keynes portrayed Wilson as a self-righteous, naive idealist who was "bamboozled" by the wily and sophisticated European politicians he met at the Peace Conference. Keynes's image of Wilson bore some resemblance to the man, but it was not entirely accurate. Nevertheless, it stuck; Wilson was never able to live it down, and it lingered in the public's mind long after his death.

American journalist William Allen White, who was present at the Peace Conference, was more sympathetic. "I cannot feel that the president is to be blamed [for failing to achieve all his goals in Paris]," wrote White. "I have seen day by day his struggle. . . . He was bound to the rocks with the vulture forever at his entrails. But they have — those damned vultures—taken the heart out of the peace."

> *They say Wilson has blundered. Perhaps he has, but I notice he usually blunders forward.*
> —JOSEPHUS DANIELS
> American journalist and politician

One of the last photographs of Wilson shows a man ravaged by illness and worn out by the burdens of office. Bitterly disappointed by America's failure to enter the League of Nations, Wilson nevertheless remained confident that, "as sure as God reigns," his goals for the nation would be achieved.

Wilson, a devoted father and grandfather, cradles his granddaughter, Ellen Wilson McAdoo. The former professor was considered proud and aloof by many contemporaries — one called him "clean, strong, high-minded, and cold-blooded" — but in his private life he was witty, affectionate, and intensely human.

In spite of the "bamboozlers" and "vultures," Wilson's achievements in Paris were tremendous. He prevented the dismemberment of Germany and reduced the insupportable financial burden the Allies wanted to impose on their conquered enemy. He secured much of what he had outlined in his Fourteen Points, including the League of Nations — even though he was finally unable to persuade the United States to join.

Wilson was hardly naive — no true "innocent" could have been elected president of the United States — but he was sincerely religious. He tried to apply his own moral standards to international politics, an arena where his talk of "purity and spiritual power" often seemed unrealistic. He was convinced that the president should be the people's leader, not merely the nation's chief executive. He thought it was the president's job to understand the hopes and dreams of America, which he believed were centered on a peaceful, secure world. As president, he set about trying to make that vision a reality.

Unquestionably an idealist, Wilson was also more — and less — than that. He has often been called a racist, and there is truth in the charge. Born in the South, raised in an atmosphere where few whites questioned their "superiority" over blacks, Wilson never lost his racial prejudice. Restaurants, public toilets, even government offices, were segregated under his administration. Addressing a group of black leaders in 1913, he said, "Segregation is not humiliating but a benefit, and ought to be so regarded by you gentlemen."

Wilson's attitude toward blacks was shared by such American leaders of the time as Theodore Roosevelt, Henry Cabot Lodge, and Nicholas Murray Butler, the distinguished educator and Nobel prize winner. Wilson's views on race, then, were not unique; neither did they do him credit.

Another fault laid to Wilson is inflexibility. Here, he can be defended. He was indeed stubborn when it came to standing up for what he believed in, but he was also a skillful politician. This meant that he could — and often did — make compromises and adjustments in order to achieve the ends he thought best for the country. His only notable exhibition of impractical stubbornness was during the struggle to get the U.S. Senate to approve the Versailles Treaty. By demanding that the treaty be approved with no modifications, he lost the prize he had worked so hard to win — U.S. membership in the League of Nations.

Both Wilson's critics and his admirers agree that he was a prophet. He insisted that if the United States did not participate in an international organization designed to prevent war, then war would occur. He was right. Just as he had predicted, World War II would indeed come, following its grim predecessor by only 21 years.

Wilson could be demanding and impatient with

> *Has justice ever grown in the soil of absolute power? Has not justice always come from the press of the heart and the spirit of men who resist power?*
> —WOODROW WILSON

those he felt were obstructing his plans. But he was also receptive to the opinions of others, and — the mark of an effective leader — was always ready to delegate responsibility. He was extremely supportive of the people he appointed to handle important jobs. Naturally reserved in crowds, he was considered

aloof and cold by many Americans. In his personal life, however, he was warm, witty, and affectionate. He was controversial in life, and his legacy has been debated in the years since his death. But few have ever doubted Woodrow Wilson's courage or his dedication to the United States, to justice, and to peace.

A painting symbolizing the unity of mankind decorates the Geneva, Switzerland, headquarters of the League of Nations — offices that later became European headquarters for the United Nations. With the founding of the UN in 1945, Wilson's enduring dream of a forum of all nations, dedicated to the preservation of peace, was finally realized.

AP/WIDE WORLD PHOTOS

Further Reading

Blum, John Morton. *Woodrow Wilson and the Politics of Morality.* Boston: Little, Brown and Company, 1956.

Cooper, John Milton Jr. *The Warrior and the Priest: Woodrow Wilson and Theodore Roosevelt.* Cambridge: The Belknap Press of Harvard University, 1983.

Cronon, E. David, ed. *The Political Thought of Woodrow Wilson.* Indianapolis: The Bobbs-Merrill Company, Inc., 1965.

Ferrell, Robert H. *Woodrow Wilson and World War I 1917–1921.* New York: Harper & Row Publishers, 1985.

Hoover, Irwin Hood. *Forty-Two Years in the White House.* Boston: Houghton Mifflin Company, 1934.

Link, Arthur S. *Woodrow Wilson and the Progressive Era 1910–1917.* New York: Harper & Row Publishers, 1954.

———. *Woodrow Wilson: Revolution, War, and Peace.* Arlington Heights, Ill.: Harlan Davidson Inc., 1979.

Tribble, Edwin, ed. *A President in Love: The Courtship Letters of Woodrow Wilson and Edith Bolling Galt.* Boston: Houghton Mifflin Company, 1981.

Chronology

Dec. 28, 1856	Born Thomas Woodrow Wilson in Staunton, Virginia
1879	Graduates from the College of New Jersey at Princeton
1885	Publishes first book, *Congressional Government* Receives Ph.D. degree from Johns Hopkins University Marries Ellen Louise Axson
1885–88	Teaches history and political economy at Bryn Mawr College
1888–90	Teaches history and government at Wesleyan University
1890	Appointed professor of jurisprudence and political economy at Princeton
1902–10	Serves as president of Princeton University
Nov. 8, 1910	Elected governor of New Jersey
Nov. 5, 1912	Elected president of the United States
Dec. 23, 1913	Signs Federal Reserve Act, providing the legal basis for the modern national banking system
1914	Outbreak of World War I in Europe; Wilson proclaims U.S. neutrality Wilson pressures Congress into passing antitrust legislation
Aug. 6, 1914	Death of Wilson's wife, Ellen Axson Wilson
Dec. 18, 1915	Wilson marries Edith Bolling Galt
Nov. 7, 1916	Reelected president
Jan. 22, 1917	Calls for "peace without victory" as the solution to the World War I conflict
April 2, 1917	Asks Congress to declare war on Germany
Jan. 8, 1918	Makes Fourteen Points speech outlining his peace plan for World War I
June 1919	Treaty of Versailles, incorporating many of the provisions outlined in Wilson's Fourteen Points, including the creation of the League of Nations, is signed by the Allies and Germany
Oct. 2, 1919	Wilson suffers a severe stroke, which leaves him partially paralyzed
Nov. 1919	U.S. Senate rejects the Versailles Treaty
March 1920	Senate rejects the Versailles Treaty a second time
1920	Wilson receives the Nobel Peace prize for 1919
1921	Term as president expires
Feb. 3, 1924	Dies in Washington, D.C.

Index

J. Perry Leavell, Jr. has taught history for many years at Drew University in Madison, New Jersey. He has written on Theodore Roosevelt and on the development of democracy in the United States.

Arthur M. Schlesinger, jr., taught history at Harvard for many years and is currently Albert Schweitzer Professor of the Humanities at City University of New York. He is the author of numerous highly praised works in American history and has twice been awarded the Pulitzer Prize. He served in the White House as special assistant to Presidents Kennedy and Johnson.

9253

B
WIL

Leavell, Perry.

Woodrow Wilson.

621944   04320D